God's People Count

About the Series

Monday Blues to Sunday Pews is a grassroots series of Christian books that will lead us on a journey through each book of the Bible, one step at a time. They will cover key verses and topics within each chapter that were life-changing then and are still life-changing today. They will inspire and encourage the "intentional" believer to move from a rut of complacency to a life that brings value to the Lord by how they live. This journey, will broaden and deepen our knowledge of God's expectations for each of us. We will learn the importance of obtaining the message from God's word and sustaining it daily through real-life application!

At the end of each chapter, as you pick up some missing nuggets in your life, you will have the opportunity to plant and share those nuggets that impacted you on our website—www.mondaybluestosundaypews.com. They will be stored like a journal and used as a testimony for others, and maybe as a reminder for you in the future. But most importantly, Monday Blues to Sunday Pews will donate over half of our proceeds to support the mission field, help the needy, and assist organizations in distributing God's word, globally. Remember this passage in Matt 16:24: *We're called to be intentional followers of Jesus Christ—daily!*

- Monday—*Meditate* on one Scripture in an area where you need help to refresh your mindset.

- Tuesday—*Tell* someone about your daily journey as you begin. Someone needs to hear it, too!

- Wednesday—*Walk* with a close friend and share your experience, as you're walking with God!

- Thursday—*Thankful* for one thing that happened this week. Showing gratitude is a huge step.

- Friday—*Focus* on another area in your life that needs improvement; we all have them.

- Saturday—*Share* one significant impact from the week with someone who also needs uplifting.

- Sunday—*Serve* in some capacity in your church or community—connect, serve, and grow.

God's People Count

Connecting God's Dots—
A Guide through the Book of Numbers

CARL BARRETT

<small>Monday Blues to Sunday Pews</small>

RESOURCE *Publications* · Eugene, Oregon

GOD'S PEOPLE COUNT
Connecting God's Dots—A Guide through the Book of Numbers

Monday Blues to Sunday Pews

Resource Publications
An Imprint of Wipf and Stock Publishers
199 W. 8th Ave., Suite 3
Eugene, OR 97401

www.wipfandstock.com

PAPERBACK ISBN: 978-1-6667-8463-3
HARDCOVER ISBN: 978-1-6667-8464-0
EBOOK ISBN: 978-1-6667-8465-7

Table of Contents

Monday Blues to Sunday Pews is a grassroots series of Christian books that will lead us on a journey through each book of the Bible, one step at a time. They will cover critical verses and topics within each chapter that were life-changing then and are still life-changing today. They will inspire and encourage the "intentional" believer to move from that rut of complacency to a life that brings value to the Lord by how they live. Through this journey, we will broaden and deepen our knowledge of God's expectations for us. We will learn the importance of obtaining the message from God's word and sustaining it daily. Real-life application!

But most importantly, Monday Blues to Sunday Pews will donate half of our profit proceeds to support the mission field, help the needy, and assist organizations in distributing God's word globally. Remember this passage in Matt. 16:24—*We're called to be intentional followers of Jesus Christ—daily!*

Monday—*Meditate* on one scripture in an area where you need help to refresh your mindset.
Tuesday—*Tell* someone about your daily journey as you begin. Someone needs to hear it, too!
Wednesday—*Walk* with a close friend and share your experience as you're walking with God!
Thursday—*Thankful* for one thing that happened this week. Showing gratitude is a huge step.
Friday—*Focus* on another area in your life that needs improvement; we all have them.
Saturday—*Share* one significant impact from the week with someone who also needs uplifting.
Sunday—*Serve* in some capacity in your church or community— connect, serve, and grow.

Biography

Carl Barrett is the Founder and Executive Director of *Monday Blues to Sunday Pews Ministry*—partnering with other Christ-based organizations globally to help the needy, support the mission field, and increase the distribution of God's word worldwide. He's the author of *God Values Our Daily Steps*, *God's Guide to Freedom*, *God's Holiness vs. Man's Lawlessness*, and *Searching for Your Comfort Zone*. In addition, he's the First Impressions Team Leader at Central Tyler Baptist Church in Tyler, Texas.

He has served as a personal development mentor for the Texas Juvenile Justice Department and teacher and preacher in multiple state penitentiaries and detention centers. He has also served as an instructor for National Fatherhood Initiative.

He holds a BSBA from Madison University. He studied biblical and theological studies at Texas Baptist Institute, "Critical Issues in Christian Apologetics" at Biola University, and "An Introduction to C.S. Lewis" at Hillsdale College. In addition, he has attended Dale Carnegie, Development Dimensions International, and Personal Dynamics Institute, where he studied human relations development, motivational leadership, and the empowerment of engagement.

Carl's aspiring passion is to help people apply the truth of God's word into their lives so they can live it out for the glory of God—as representatives of Jesus Christ on this earth. He would tell you that it starts in our homes—then throughout our neighborhoods, community, church home, and abroad. *Our bio as Christlike followers is essential to our Lord and the building of His Kingdom in our everyday life!*

The Common Ground

The New Mexico State Penitentiary near Santa Fe, New Mexico, is one of the most hardened and dangerous prisons in the United States. It is the site of one of the most egregious prison riots in U.S. history. It's known (by some reports) as one of the worst penal institutions for riots among inmates—and even attacks on the correction officers because they are always at odds.[1]

On these grounds, in the early morning of February 2, 1980, a nightmare began to unfold where inmates took over the facility for a day and a half. What would proceed left its horrific mark on people, a community, the state, and the country. While some prisoners tried to find a safe place to wait out the riot, others banded together to rampage through the Old Main Unit, torturing and murdering other inmates—because they were on a mission to seek and destroy.

What happened over thirty-six hours would be recorded as one of New Mexico's bloodiest events in the past century, and today, its effects still linger. This riot changed everything we knew about the scariness of things behind prison walls—because this occurrence rattled and shook people to the core of their souls.

The apparent caution signs and red flags seemed to be avoided and ignored by officials. The inmates continuously cried out and tried to tell them there was too much overcrowding, unsanitary conditions, and improperly housing violent and non-violent offenders in the same cells. They were also upset with the cancellation of prison programs that many found beneficial in their rehabilitation. There was apparently a significant disconnect between the inmates and prison officials, leading to division, chaos, and utter destruction.

This violent act would leave thirty-three inmates murdered and twelve officers held captive. At one point during this riot, men during the night were slaughtered, dissected, and quickly burned; most of them were child molesters. The inmates who conspired in this evil act had a code and motive

---

1. Hanson, "The 20 Worst Prisons in America."

of vengeance. Several men they targeted in this premeditated attack were snitches and abusers.

Inmates alleged to be betrayers were also tortured, mutilated, and burned alive. Others were killed for grudges held by other inmates, and hundreds more were injured. Guards who encouraged snitching and engaged in beatings also faced retaliation as they were held hostage. The images of burned men with a blowtorch have left their evil depictions and graphic images in the old compound that still stands today, forty-three years later.

What took place in this institution is due to the corruption of man's sin, which is a state of decay, pollution, incorrectness, and a complete disconnect from God and His word. When we're not connected to the common ground of a Holy God, it can lead to moral contamination and spiritual perish because of our disobedience toward His ways. Therefore, like many people and organizations in this country, this facility needed God and a complete transformation! He was the only One who could do this through the power of His word and the Holy Spirit. But the key was this—they had to be connected with God!

And it is here, in this same penitentiary, where the Lord called me in my first years of service as a mentor in the prison ministry. The detailed training that I went through—and learning all the do's and don'ts provided me with some insight into "what to do—and what not to do." But when you go inside a compound of this magnitude—all alone—and once those steel doors slam shut with a sound permeating through the thick concrete walls, it sends goosebumps up and down your spine and shakes you to the core of your soul. As I write this, I can still hear it, see it, and even smell it to this day—because the scents and presence in a prison are unlike anything known to the average person on the streets.

How would the Lord use one man with very little training as a mentor within this compound—with over 600 inmates? Little did I know, and I should have known this, but when God has your back, trust me, He has your back! When you're connected to the power of His Spirit, and you humbly give it to Him and make it all about His works (and not you), He protects you and provides you with the words, strength, protection, and faith to endure and persevere. He does this because He knows that your heart, motives, and desires are intended for His glory. It was all about my solid relationship with the Lord during these years of service. Through His empowering grace, He enabled me to connect out of calmness and confidence.

I assisted the Chaplain in this massive facility by going around each cell, one at a time, passing out Christian material, and trying to get the inmates to open up and engage. The key was this—connecting with them in a productive spiritual conversation. But at the same time—and this was vital—building trust, confidence, realness, and dependability. Because most of their life, these are critical components the inmates did not possess with anyone.

I have always thought of myself as gregarious and engaging with the gift of gab. So, I automatically expected to connect with everyone in an open conversation—from the start. That was a big NOT! One thing I learned was this. In many of the pods, which comprised twelve cells (six above and six below), I was being monitored and scoped by many of these highly skilled, intelligent, and even dangerous prisoners.

Here's what they were observing. Was I consistently coming every week? In other words, was I faithful and reliable as a mentor? Was my message positive and concise, and what was the level of my tone? Did they see any merit in the content of my message? Was I listening more than talking? What was the demeanor of my body language? Did I have a posture of man's fear—or absolute faith and boldness in Almighty God? Did they see me as a sanctimonious, self-righteous, and holier-than-thou mentor who thought he knew it all? This was important to them because they were looking for someone genuine and authentic—"the real deal." Not a phony!

Inside their cells, they had all the time in the world to craft their skills to the max. After all, many were incarcerated 24-7, with no liberty. They read a lot, took correspondence courses in law, physics, world history, and religion, and became scholars—in their own right. Many of them could create things with very little material for their personal use in the cells, such as a device called a stinger, which was used to warm their coffee. They could make deadly weapons with a 6" wire, soap, and toilet paper. Their demeanor and voices were enough to intimidate the most formidable man. They had no fear of anyone, including the guards. I would say that they were jack of all trades—and mastered them all!

Over time, many men wanted to talk, but quite a few stared at me with the glare of death. They wanted nothing to do with me as a Christian—they despised and hated my message and probably me! They did not see any common ground with me as a mentor and sent a profound message through their body language that there would never be a connection. Let's face it; physically, emotionally, and mentally, I did not connect with inmates affiliated with the Mexican Mafia, Crips and Bloods, and the Cartel. And many of them were atheists, Satanists, Muslims, and various other beliefs. The Chaplain even told me to stay away from certain inmates because they could have my family killed if they wanted to—they were that connected to the underworld on the outside. In their little world, some of these prisoners had equal power, if not more, than the President of the United States.

Do you sense the fear that could rattle anyone's spiritual cage from wanting to serve in this type of ministry? However, I had one source that could connect us spiritually! By His power, He would give me the grace to persevere through those most challenging days and never fear the mere mortal man. I cannot count the times I quoted these scriptures in my heart and mind; 'I can do all things through Christ, which strengthens me" (Phil 4:13), "If God is for us, who can be against us" (Rom 8:31), "The name of the Lord is a strong fortress; the godly run to him and are safe" (Prov 18:10), "The Lord is my light and my salvation—so why should I be afraid?" (Ps 27:1), and "For we are not fighting against flesh-and-blood enemies, but against evil rulers and authorities of the unseen world" (Eph 6:12). Truly, the word of God is our stronghold and sword in everyday life. I needed and longed for the connecting power of the Holy Spirit and His word every time I walked inside those prison walls!

As in life, I wanted everyone to like me and open up, but that was not to be. There were certain men that I wanted to talk with, but they would not give me the light of day. There was one man in particular; his name was Joe. When I first met him, he made it clear that he did not want to talk with me. Whenever I entered his pod, he would turn off his light in the 7' x 11' cell and even cover up his 3" x 18" window with a towel.

However, I walked by his darkened cell every week, hoping this would be the day. There were days of discouragement, but for whatever reason, I felt the Lord leading me to talk with Joe. Man, you talk about patience; I needed it because this lingered for approximately six months—but it seemed like an eternity!

And it was in that least expected moment when I visited Joe's pod—I walked by his cell, and there he stood waiting for me, all 6'4" and 230 pounds, covered with tattoos from his neck to his ankles, with hardly any body fat. At first glance, he was an intimidating force to look at. He stared down at me from his small window in the cell and said these profound words; "I've been watching and observing you and listening to the tone and message of your conversations with other inmates over the past several months. You seem like someone I can trust and talk with." Do you see the operative words in his statement? They want people to talk "with them," "not to them."

So often, the only way to capture that common ground with another person is to bring your conversation to eye level "with them"—spiritually and emotionally. When we discover those areas of mutual interest, they can open up unbelievable doors of communication that will enable us to connect with anyone in life.

When Christians share their testimony from the heart, it is one of the best ways to find common ground with a non-believer or anyone who may be struggling. Our life-changing testimony is simply the story of what Christ has done in our life. And in so many cases, Jesus is precisely what others seek, especially in times of hopelessness, helplessness, and loneliness—because they have a void that must be filled!

I was so ecstatic that I finally connected with Joe. I thought I had just hit the lottery! There was no amount of money you could have given me to replace the value and joy of this openness I longed for with this one inmate. Over time, as he progressed through the system, we became close friends. At one time, I thought Joe was my enemy, but the power of God turned this into a relationship that I treasure to this day!

One day, we had an open conversation; I asked him what had finally led him to open up with me. He said, "I overheard your testimony with some of the inmates, and then I knew there was a common ground between you and me." This mutual interest would eventually bond us as brothers. Regardless of my title or position as a Mentor or Assistant to the Chaplain, he realized that my life's testimony had many parallels with even a hardened prisoner in a state penitentiary!

I discovered Joe was at the time thirty-five and had been in and out of halfway houses, orphanages, juvenile detention, and prisons since the age of thirteen. He did not know his parents and had little recollection of family and friends! He was definitely a loner, and the prison was his connector in life! The outside world was not his life of comfort; it was the life inside those prison walls where he felt at ease.

It's not that I was trying to act fictitiously in luring Joe to talk with me—it is what the Lord was doing in my life in being honest, humble, and genuine, which led to powerful spiritual connections. And I am here to tell you that if humility and judging others falsely is an area of your life that you struggle with, pray about it and volunteer to serve in a ministry that can bring life to a "real" perspective—and will alter your attitude toward God's creation.

Trust me when I say, "Looks of perceiving can be deceiving." What I mean is this. When we perceive any prisoner as evil because of their one wrong choice, we must remind ourselves that we all make bad choices. Perception and reality are completely different, but perception can influence how we look at reality. And we should be careful because here's the difference.

In our finite minds, humans see a person in a small cell serving a lifetime sentence for one wrong choice. We perceive them as evil, forever lost, and say, "Lock them in the darkest and deepest cell and throw away the key." However, on the other side of the coin, God, who is infinite and all-knowing, and all-powerful, can enforce the power of reality when His love, mercy, and grace can lead one prisoner to make "one right choice" that can change the whole course of their heavenly and eternal life.

What happened in that state prison over four years is unexplainable—because it was the supernatural power of God. Men incarcerated for some of the most unspeakable crimes known to humankind came to know, believe, and accept Christ as their Savior. We were baptizing men in horse troughs filled with water and lined with garbage bags. One gentleman who was one of only two men on death row in the state (before the death penalty was abolished in New Mexico) is now teaching Sunday School in this prison. The ministry was so powerful that there were times when the Correction Officers would open the port doors and allow me to hold hands with prisoners and pray with them.

As I shared my story as a mentor in this penitentiary with others, many told me I was crazy! They said, "They could have pulled your arm in and slit you," but I must tell you that never crossed my mind. I was in God's hands of protection. I look back now, and there's no doubt—that God had His Almighty Hands over me during those wonderful years of service. And this preparation would lead me to serve Him in that same capacity and preach and teach in other prisons over the years.

What was the key? By the grace of God, He enabled me to remove self, act out humility, lean upon His power, and be an open book, sharing my life experiences in a raw sense, which is precisely what these inmates needed to hear. Prisoners are about as raw and genuine as they come, and they were looking for that same connector in life.

Over the years, I've seen murderers, rapists, child molesters, thieves, gangbangers, drug dealers, Muslims, and Satanists accept Christ as their Savior. Once they connect with their Lord, Savior, and Redeemer, you see their life-changing experience spread throughout the prison walls. It is profound because it not only changes them and others but you, too! Discovering that common ground with another person can lead to an unbelievable relationship and solid foundation with Christ. It can be a soul-saver because everyone counts in God's eyes!

While we know, unfortunately, that every person will not be saved, 1 Tim 2:4–6 reminds us that God, our Savior, wants everyone to be saved and to understand the truth, for there is one God and one Mediator who can reconcile God and humanity—and that is the man Christ Jesus. He gave his life to purchase freedom for everyone, including that one inmate in a small, dark cell.

And 2 Pet 3:9 sums it up perfectly, "The Lord is not slow in keeping his promise; instead, he is patient with you, not wanting anyone to perish, but everyone to come to repentance." Our job and responsibility as Christ-followers are to discover that common ground and connect with people who may be lost.

Jesus reminds us in Matt 18:10-14, "Beware that you don't look down on any of these little ones, for I tell you that in heaven, their angels are always in the presence of my heavenly Father. "If a man has a hundred sheep, and one of them wanders away, what will he do? Won't he leave the ninety-nine others on the hills and go out to search for the one that is lost? And if he finds it, I tell you the truth, he will rejoice over it more than over the ninety-nine that didn't wander away! In the same way, it is not my heavenly Father's will that even one of these little ones should perish."

Just like the shepherd's concern over that one lost sheep, so is our Heavenly Father's concern about every human being He created—they all count and matter to Him. So, if we encounter anyone in our community who is lost, discover that common ground and use words and acts of lovingkindness that will connect you with them. Because in so many cases, godly actions will always prove to be that one way of connecting with people, which can make a life-saving difference. If one matters in the eyes of God, that one person within your proximity, no matter who they are, what they've done, or where they live, should matter to us, too!

> Phil 4:8, "And now, dear brothers and sisters, one final thing. Fix your thoughts on what is true, and honorable, and right, and pure, and lovely, and admirable. Think about things that are excellent and worthy of praise."
>
> Col 3:1–2, "Since you have been raised to new life with Christ, set your sights on the realities of heaven, where Christ sits in the place of honor at God's right hand. Think about the things of heaven, not the things of earth."

Preface

We are undoubtedly living in a society and culture that is growing stranger by the day—creating more distance between others, minute by minute. It seems that people are living in their own little bubbles and silos more than ever—with no interest in connecting with people effectively. And it is evident that the rise of the digital age is affecting people mentally and emotionally, leading to voidness and isolation.

There are millions of people today who are overwhelmed with the state of loneliness, hopelessness, and helplessness. They focus more on their pasts than the blessings that they possess today! Billions of people globally are connecting with an unproductive device in their hands when it should be the word of God! There is no spiritual value when we allow the things of this world to consume our lives more than God's divine nature. Do we really think anything will improve in our homes, communities, churches, schools, country, and globally if we're not grounded in the Truths of His word?

In an article on Dave Ramsey's site, Dr. John Delony, a mental health expert, said in this article entitled "The Importance of Human Connection," "Many Western countries are facing a social epidemic that's devastating for our well-being. Simply put: Loneliness is killing us. The stress of disconnection contributes to addiction, ADHD, anxiety, depression, heart disease, obesity, and suppressed immune systems, just to name a few. We must work to make this right immediately, for the stakes are too high!" [1] Because sadly, digital interactions are skyrocketing, and the scary fact is this; data shows we're losing human connection in everyday life.

Millions of us have one thousand "friends" online, but there is not one person within our proximity who can help us with a dire situation because we are not effectively connected with people. We must realize that connecting with humans physically, emotionally, and spiritually is how God designed us. Just like our Creator wants a relationship with you and me, He wants us to

1. Delony, "Importance of Human Connection."

bond with others so they can also see the experience of His abundant blessings and goodness in our lives.

Human connection is physical, eye-to-eye, intimate, intentional, sharing emotions, genuine personal care, setting everything down in our personal lives, and extending grace, love, and forgiveness. In other words, we embrace, engage, and get involved in people's lives. We cannot afford to be on the sidelines because it's all about cultivating genuine care for God's creation and putting it into practice for the sake of ourselves and others.

A real connection is like scuba diving: You cannot stay on the surface if you want to have rich and meaningful relationships. You must dive in and get wet and sometimes go deep! But we must remember that connecting with others is a choice, like everything else in life. If you need help in this area, it is much easier to discover common ground or mutual interests with someone first because it will help you open up the communication line.

I wrote a self-help book over twenty years ago, "Searching For Your Comfort Zone." The main point of this book was to show the reader how to escape from feeling uncomfortable when working with their customer. It was designed to help them establish an ease by "first understanding and knowing the customer's needs." When we ascertain the knowledge of understanding things first, we can then build a solid relationship.

But the nuts and bolts of the book were for the student to instill a quality of conduct and characteristics in their life that would bring value and respect, which the customer would treasure. And when that was established, the relationship started to reciprocate.

So often in life, we don't communicate with others because it takes us out of our comfort zone. And that's mainly because we don't know how to approach a person and have no grasp on the first thing we should say. I firmly believe that when we try to force something unnaturally, it will not lead to anything productive.

However, as Christians, when we lean upon God's supernatural power, He can enable our gifts through His Spirit to help us approach others more openly and genuinely. And when we trust in His empowering grace, our relationship with the Lord is intact vertically, and everything falls horizontally in place. Our steadfast faith, boldness, and confidence come to the surface, and we will not miss out on any failed opportunities to share our life-changing stories.

When that happens, our flesh will not force our choice of words, but they will flow from Him like second nature. One of the best ways to open the door of communication with anyone is if Christians would display a genuine disposition of humility, joy, gentleness, kindness, compassion, grace, patience, and cooperation. When we allow the Holy Spirit to be at full use in our Christian lives, He will illuminate and exhibit these qualities that will open doors in glorious ways!

The power of connection is needed in every part of our daily life. Parents need to bond with their children, husband and wife need to be united, teenagers need healthy relationships, employers and employees need trusting ties, teachers and students need to be engaged, neighbors in a community need to be supportive of each other, we all need trusting confidantes in our personal lives, Christians need to connect spiritually and effectively with their church, and most importantly we need a binding tie with our Heavenly Father through Jesus Christ.

If there is a disconnect in any way, shape, or form in the above areas, we can get disjointed, and friction, chaos, confusion, and division can occur. We must realize that healthy connections are vital—and could be the universal and most dynamic topic overlooked in everyday life. But there will never be a connection with groups or individuals unless there is an "established common ground or mutual interest" between the two parties. That's why unity in the body of Christ is so vital in today's time of disarray.

And the key component that links these all together is Christlike love, better known as Agape love! God's word reminds us in Col 3:14, "And above all these put on love, which binds everything together in perfect harmony." Of all the virtues Paul mentioned, none was as crucial as Christlike love, for it is the one godly attribute that binds all things together. To implement or practice any list of virtues without enforcing divine love will only lead to distortion and stagnation. In other words, it will not be productive.

In 1 Corinthians chapter thirteen, better known as the love chapter, God tells us here that love is the greatest of all human qualities in life because it's an attribute of God's divine nature. Only three things will remain through the test of time: faith, hope, and love, and the greatest of all these is love! And this type of love involves unselfish service, setting self on the shelf, and putting God's qualities in motion. And the key to putting God's love in action for everyone is when our faith and hope align with Him! When we understand this wholly, we can act as our Lord does.

Without genuine "agape" love, we will not connect or even make efforts to try and find common ground with anyone. God's word tells us that without His love at work in our lives, we will not possess the desire or drive to unite spiritually with others. We must realize it is the foundation and building block to a genuine godly connection; without it, our efforts will be futile.

Jesus Christ even reinforces the power of connection and common ground, which starts with Him. He reminds us powerfully in John chapter fifteen that He is the True Vine, and as genuine believers, we are the branch connected to Him, and apart from this True Vine, we cannot accomplish anything. He said that no branch could even live, let alone produce leaves and fruit, by itself—because if the branch is cut off from the trunk, it is dead. This illustration of the Vine and branches is a stark reality and tells us of the importance of connection.

Just as we know that a healthy living tree produces good fruit, we also recognize that fruitless and useless branches have no connection to the True Vine; this is why Jesus tells us, "By their fruit, you will know them" (Matthew 7:16–20). Those who do not produce good fruit are cut away and burned. And what we need to understand in this passage is that our common ground with the Lord is the fruit we bear. If we don't bear any fruit, we will not have a genuine connection or mutual interest with Jesus Christ. [2]

The great apostle Paul tells us in 2 Corinthians chapter nine the importance of establishing common ground with others. And when we apply these basic principles in our life, they can open the gateway of communication in sharing the Good News. In these passages, he gives several essential principles for ministry. 1) Find common ground with those you contact, 2) Avoid a know-it-all attitude, 3) Make others feel accepted, 4) Be sensitive to their needs and concerns, and 5) Look for opportunities to tell them about Christ.

Paul is laying the foundation for connecting with others in powerful ways. We must remember that our approach of genuineness, humility, empathy, gentleness, and lovingkindness is critical to establishing that common ground so people will feel comfortable and confident with us as believers. This does not happen by email, text, or phone calls but by getting out in the field of ministry and telling the world that there is Great News of truth that promises hope for the future. And at just the right time, when our genuine Christlikeness is constantly on display, there will be a person who wants to connect with you and me.

As ambassadors and messengers for Christ, we must realize this key factor: Whatever we connect with daily can sway our emotions—one way or another. So, be careful about "what our eyes see and what our ears hear" because that one person we're trying to establish a Christlike bond with could be affected if we get off course. And if anything, we never want to be a stumbling block in someone's life.

We don't want our mindsets and hearts to be lured to the bad, harmful, toxic, non-productive or barriers in life. Instead, we should aspire to surround ourselves with spiritually productive things. This is important because these attributes or vices could influence and determine our effectiveness in how we

2. 'What Did Jesus Mean when He Said, I Am the True Vine?"

connect with God and others. As Christians, it's our responsibility to ensure that what we look at and listen to is good, positive, encouraging, safe, and beneficial—while building up the body of Christ.

They say that our eyes are the window to our soul. This famous phrase is related to the Bible verses found in Matt 6:22–24 which says, "Your eye is like a lamp that provides light for your body. When your eye is healthy, your whole body is filled with light. But when your eye is unhealthy, your whole body is filled with darkness. And if the light you think you have is actually darkness, how deep that darkness is! "No one can serve two masters. For you will hate one and love the other; you will be devoted to one and despise the other. You cannot serve God and be enslaved to money."

In this sense, our eyes represent our life's focus and what we seek and want to connect with more of now and in the future. If we chase after money and the everyday pleasures of life rather than the love and truth of God, we will ultimately find despair and heartache. God desires us to do and see the world from His point of view, which requires you and me to have a spiritual vision of seeing things through His lenses. If our eyes and hearts are not connected with Him spiritually, our vision will be obscured, and we will pursue other interests that will block our godly views and disconnect us from God.

Throughout scripture, we see the power and benefit of people connecting with God after establishing a common ground with Him. Just look at the stories of Noah, Abraham, Jacob, Moses, Joshua, David, Rahab, Esther, Ruth, Ezekiel, Isaiah, Jeremiah, Daniel, Paul, John, Peter, and James (to name a few). Their common ground of love, faith, obedience, humility, and willingness to serve their God connected these faithful servants with their Lord, which led to a more deep-hearted and solid relationship! They were always willing to put their gifts to use for His glory.

After all, since the beginning of time, God said it was not good for us to be alone (Gen 2:18)—so, He established relationships. But what we gain, learn, and experience from spiritually healthy relationships reflects the kind of connection God wants to have with us. That happens when we're on the same common ground with our Heavenly Father, which is the awe and reverence that is appropriate for coming into His place of worship and praise. And one of the most instrumental ways of connecting with our Lord is when we're utilizing our God-given gifts for His glory. These abilities are the common ground with our Heavenly Father because they produce the fruit He desires daily.

Examples: Many of you have the gift of using words with grace and love that could bring someone from their bottomless pit to unbelievable heights of joy and hope. Some of you have the incredible knack of writing words on paper so powerfully and eloquently that they can strike an inner core with anyone—especially that person who could be in a dire situation. Many of you have undeniable acts of generosity, hospitality, lovingkindness, and goodness. If you thought those acts could affect one person's life, would you change your outlook as a servant?

So many of you have crafts and skills to help people who need some type of repair. That use of your talent and skill could connect you with that one right person at God's appointed time. Many have ascertained an unbelievable breadth of wisdom and knowledge of God's word. But are we using this depth of comprehension for the fruitful benefit of building His Kingdom? How are we connecting the dots of what God's endowed us by helping others?

If we know beyond a shadow of a doubt that our calling in this life is of service to one another—as Christ commands, what would we change in our daily actions? So many of us don't realize the potential we possess that could be significant and essential to others in need—especially for the glory of God. If we did, it might change our perspective on how we can help others in this life journey.

Just how important is God's creation of humans to you and me? No matter who they are, what they've done, or where they live, what steps have we taken to connect with that person who needs it now? Have we attempted to discover that common ground that could open the door of communication? When we truly understand how much God values you and me, maybe that will open our hearts to the "value of relationships" through God's eyes! Remember, relationships are for God's glory—because that one connecting dot counts in the eyes of God!

Introduction

One of the top TV shows of all time was Andy Griffith, and many of you may remember that one episode when a stranger named Ed Sawyer moved to Mayberry from a local town. As Ed moves in, he asks Andy for help. He explains how Mayberry became his "hometown," revealing that he's a loner with no family and no real home. He was looking for a community of people he could be associated with in everyday life.

It seems that, in the army, Ed befriended Joe Larson from Mayberry (son of Pete and Edie Larson). He loved the stories Joe told about "back home" so much that he began to take the town newspaper and would tell folks he was from Mayberry. Over time, he became very familiar with all the key people in Mayberry; he knew almost everything about their lives.

As he settles in and becomes comfortable, he walks the streets of that town consistently, displaying the most charming smile and positive outlook on life. He made every effort to connect with the people through his loving and kind acts. But unfortunately, it did not work.

In all his attempts to find common ground with the townspeople, he could never connect with them because he did not possess that genuine personal and intimate relationship with the community. Outwardly, he thought he did, but that was not the case. So, the people rejected him, and in one scene, Ed is confronted by a frightened, angry crowd who wants to run him out of town.

Andy (Sheriff) tells Ed's story and delivers a stern lecture to many citizens about how to treat people who may appear to be a bit different. Andy told the townspeople that Ed moved to Mayberry because he had read and heard that this was a community of friendly and genuine people. Once the people heard this, their perspective shifted. The once-angry mob backs down and welcomes their new neighbor to Mayberry. All it took was one key person— Andy, the Sheriff of the community, to defend Ed because he knew his motives were genuine and from the heart. And this significant point is the only thing that mattered to Andy.

In life, just like Ed, we all need to feel noticed, valued, appreciated, recognized, accepted, our voice heard, needed, loved, comforted, supported, motivated, and desired; and see eye to eye with one another. We need to laugh with, talk and listen to, be open and honest with, and trust someone who can help us. Sometimes connection is a heart-to-heart, lay all the cards on the table, and spill-it-all-out talk. But sometimes, it's just a laugh-out-loud e-mail, phone call, or text.

I think we could all admit that what gets us through some of our most fierce life challenges is those genuine connections with our loved ones, close friends, family members, and brothers and sisters in Christ! We all need those invaluable relationships with someone who can help us overcome our hurdles in life.

But to have that type of solid relationship, there is one dimension that must be accomplished, and that is the power and act of connecting. Undoubtedly, it is one of humankind's most exciting, reciprocating, and interesting dimensions because it can lead to unbelievable heights of joy and pleasure.

Poor Ed had to work extra hard to get the people in Mayberry to finally accept him. But guess what? Someone is out there, whether a friend, family member, neighbor, brother, sister in Christ, or even a stranger, who needs to connect with someone because they are in a dire circumstance!

Matt 25:37-40, "Then these righteous ones will reply, 'Lord, when did we ever see you hungry and feed you? Or thirsty and give you something to drink? Or a stranger and show you hospitality? Or naked and give you clothing? When did we ever see you sick or in prison and visit you?' "And the King will say, 'I tell you the truth, when you did it to one of the least of these, my brothers and sisters, you were doing it to me!'"

When the core of this passage is lived in and through us, we will make a difference in people's lives. We will reveal genuine acts of mercy and love when we seek and act on the power of connection with God's creation. Remember, our Lord, Jesus Christ, demands our personal involvement in caring for others, especially those in need. God needs us to connect with others today because many are straying away from society, leading them to loneliness and hopelessness.

God's word reminds us in Matt 9:35-38, "Jesus traveled through all the towns and villages of that area, teaching in the synagogues, and announcing the Good News about the Kingdom. And he healed every kind of disease and illness. When he saw the crowds, he had compassion on them because they were confused and helpless, like sheep without a shepherd. He said to his disciples, "The harvest is great, but the workers are few. So, pray to the Lord who is in charge of the harvest; ask him to send more workers into his fields."

In this passage, Jesus is telling you and me that He needs us to help people deal with various life problems. He expects us to comfort others by showing them the experiences of God's blessings and goodness in our own lives. This shows others that we're just as human as they are, and we've been through life's difficulties, too. We can tell them that God can help them like He did for you and me; it can lift others up in powerful ways for God's glory. This cannot happen if we don't connect genuinely with others!

We must connect with others as the triune (Father, Son, and Holy Spirit) is connected. Our Heavenly Father and Creator established common ground with us through His Son, Jesus Christ, and left us with the power of the Holy Spirit to help us in every area of our Christian walk. Jesus reminds us profoundly in John 17:10, "All I have is yours, and all you have is mine. And glory has come to me through them."

One of the most beautiful depictions of our Savior Jesus connecting with His disciples is recorded in John 13:12-17, where He taught them a lesson when He washed each of their feet. He was not only washing their feet to show them His lowly service of humility and how to express that lovingkindness to others, but His greater illustration was to expand His mission and God's plan on earth after He was gone.

Christ's followers were to go into the world and serve their Father, serve each other and all the people to whom they would preach salvation. This can only happen if His disciples connect with the people and seek common ground to accomplish this mission. They would find common ground in areas of agreement—but also biblically correct others when there were areas of disagreement with grace and love. This could only be done by the guidance of God's word and the Holy Spirit.

But also, in finding common ground with the people, they would never compromise their core godly values or agree with the ways of the world. It was their stance in all Christ's teachings and adherence to it 100%. In doing so, the truth would be revealed, and through faith in Jesus Christ, new believers would extend the same service to others.

God's word reminds us in 2 Tim 3:16–17, "All Scripture is inspired by God and is useful to teach us what is true and to make us realize what is wrong in our lives. It corrects us when we are wrong and teaches us to do what is right. God uses it to prepare and equip his people to do every good work."

Jesus knew how to take the initiative and respond to people. He almost always met people on their own turf, and our Lord was interested in establishing common ground with others. Just look at the examples of His connecting with the tax collectors and sinners (Matt 9:9–13), with the Samaritan woman (John 4:7–42), the crippled beggar (John 5:1-15), an adulterous woman (John

8:8–11), a rich young ruler (Matt 19:16–30) and even His disciples when He first commissioned them. Jesus asked questions in more than half of His conversations and knew how to connect with people's most inner thoughts and feelings. Our Lord and Savior is the example we must follow in connecting with people who need Him today! This is vital!

Because many people in this society are not connected with a body of believers, and they desperately need someone in their life today. Millions of people in this country and globally have a dull spiritual life—or no belief at all. They are searching for help and answers because they have succumbed to the ways of the world that are leading them down ungodly paths.

So many within our own proximity need purpose, meaning, clarity, hope, help, refining, and molding into the ways of Jesus Christ. And that starts with you and me connecting with people—so we can help those who are hurting in many ways. God's word tells us in Prov 27:17, "As iron sharpens iron, so a friend sharpens a friend."

We were not created to be alone, especially after the Fall of Man, because the enemy is out to seek and destroy more now than ever. God implores us to come together with our brothers and sisters in Christ for seasons of fellowship and prayer. This was recognized by the early church saints (Acts 2:42–47), who "devoted themselves" to teaching, fellowship, communion, and prayer, all corporate activities that provided opportunities for sharpening one another.

When we are surrounded by faithful followers of Christ, we will walk away with more mental and spiritual sharpness and awareness, ready to serve our Lord faithfully. And trust me, there is someone out there that needs to be a part of this type of family! As God's connected servants on Earth with Christ, here's the sweet spot we are all looking for—"Connection is being fully known and fully loved—from that vertical relationship that reciprocates horizontally."[1] And we all need that type of connection so we can spread it!

As we journey through the Book of Numbers, it will show us the importance of discovering God's common ground of holiness—and how to connect with Him in ways that will enrich our lives and others for His glory.

1. Delony, "The Importance of Human Connection."

The Book of Numbers

Let us now embark on a journey through the Book of Numbers. What we will see in this beautiful book is the continual unbelief of God's chosen nation, Israel. God has always wanted the best for His children, and He showed them through the faithfulness of His promises, provisions, and protection that He should always be trusted.

But regardless of their unbelief, God demonstrated His incredible mercy and patience because, time after time, He withholds His judgment, and instead, He preserves the nation. However, just like us today, when we continuously disobey and take His love, mercy, and grace for granted, His judgment will come.

In the book of Numbers, the nation of Israel is still camped at the foot of Mount Sinai, where they have received God's laws—and He's preparing them to move forward to the promised land. First, a census would be taken to determine the number of men fit for military service. Then the people were set apart, and God would make them spiritually and physically ready to receive their inheritance. In this book, we will see the importance of the Israelites staying connected to God; if not, they would not be ready to move when He commanded.

This book depicts an excellent example of the importance of unity with God and being a part of His plan. It was when the twelve spies were sent to the land of Canaan to assess its strength—we all know the story oh so well. Ten spies returned with fearful accounts of giants, while two men filled with the Spirit and connected with the power of God; Joshua and Caleb encouraged them to go at once and take the land that God had promised.

What did these two men possess that the other ten and the nation did not have? Absolute faith and trust in God. However, because these two were the minority, their report fell on deaf ears. The present generation's unbelief in a Sovereign God would prevent them from seeing the Promise Land; what a missed opportunity! And this led to their disconnect from God and years of wandering in the wilderness.

Throughout this book is a continual and habitual pattern of complaining, moaning, groaning, grumbling, discontentment, unfaithfulness, and disobedience. And these harmful vices prevented them from establishing that common ground with their Almighty God. And because of this disconnect with Yahweh, there would be a long waiting period for the old generation to die off. But as the old generation perishes, we will see if the new generation will faithfully obey God and connect with Him in all His ways.

This book reveals how God reminded Israel that He would not tolerate their rebellion, complaining, and disbelief without invoking consequences. He taught His people how to walk with Him—not just with their feet through the wilderness but with their mouths in worship, hands in service, and lives as witnesses to the surrounding nations. He was their God, they were His people, and He expected them to act like it. And this could only happen if they were genuinely united with Him.

The book will end as it began, with preparation because the new generation of Israelites was counted and set apart for God's use. After defeating numerous armies, they settled on the Jordan River's east side. And then the time was coming when they would be confronted with their most crucial test: crossing the Jordan River and possessing the land of milk and honey God had promised.

Will God's people move when He says move? Will they trust and obey Him every step of the way? They could only claim the land if they faithfully relied upon God and all His guidance. Just like the Israelites, if we allow the vices of the world and the enemy to prevent us from connecting with God, we can and will miss the undeniable blessings He has in store for you and me.

When we're not focused on God's common ground, and we're drifting away from Him, it's likely due to these areas of opportunity; 1) A lack of communication, which is our prayer life. 2) We're not consistently and faithfully in His word and looking for those areas of weaknesses that we need to turn into strengths—and seizing those opportunities of service. 3) We're harboring frustration and anger, keeping us in the wandering wilderness because we're more divisive than united. 4) We've lost the love of genuine fellowship and worship with our Lord. That's critical to staying connected daily. 5) We're straddling the fence as if we're more lukewarm than "all in for the Lord." Remember, there's no middle ground with the Lord. We must dive in wholeheartedly. 6) We're connected to more worldly devices than those of God. When we allow this to happen, it yields no spiritual value in our Christlike walk. And 7) We complain, groan, and grumble more—than rejoice, encourage, and be more positive.

God's word reminds us in Galatians chapter five that Christ died to set us free from sin and a long list of laws and regulations. He came to this earth to redeem and free us and reconcile our connection and relationship with God the Father. This does not mean we have the freedom to do whatever our flesh desires. Instead, our common ground with Jesus Christ is genuine saving faith, demonstrating our devotion out of love and commitment to His ways, not the ways of the world.

When we're connected to the Holy Spirit and the power of God's word, we're living under the liberty of Jesus Christ that yields the by-products of the Fruit of the Spirit in our daily lives (from love through self-control, Gal 5:22–23). But when we're held captive under the flesh and disconnected from God's ways, we're in bondage and can drift away.

Our ongoing connection with God is beautifully depicted in Psalm Chapter 1. When our roots are grounded and connected like sturdy trees planted by streams of water that bear fruit, this is the type of life that pleases our Lord. "Oh, the joys of those who do not follow the advice of the wicked, or stand around with sinners, or join in with mockers. But they delight in the law of the Lord, meditating on it day and night. They are like trees planted along the riverbank, bearing fruit each season. Their leaves never wither, and they prosper in all they do."

God wants to connect with us in powerful ways through His word and Spirit, so we will seek those common grounds with the most unlikely person and get them connected with the One who may need Christ today. Jesus emphasized the importance of staying connected with the Father and his disciples, and that is why Jesus asked us to stay connected with Him. He tells us in John 15:4 to remain in Him and abide in Him, and He will abide in us—for without that connection, our efforts will be futile.

God's word reminds us in Heb 4:12–13, "For the word of God is alive and powerful. It is sharper than the sharpest two-edged sword, cutting between soul and spirit, between joint and marrow. It exposes our innermost thoughts and desires. Nothing in all creation is hidden from God. Everything is naked and exposed before his eyes, and he is the one to whom we are accountable."

God knows everything about you and me and sees all our actions in word and deed. He expects followers of Jesus Christ to imitate His Son in every area of our daily life, and there is no way we can hide from our Sovereign God. His powerful words challenge us to live out our Christlike life in a manner that will spread His word to others—so we can connect with people in ways that will enable them to connect with Him.

God desires an eternal relationship with anyone who accepts His Son, Jesus Christ, by faith. And that invitation can only happen unless you and I connect the unbelieving world with the Good News of Jesus Christ. The angels in Heaven rejoice over that one person accepting Christ as their Savior. Just think about that for a moment. You and I have the unbelievable opportunity to help the angels rejoice if we would only connect with that one person who needs the Lord today. Connecting with others can significantly impact people's lives, and it starts with you and me!

Rev 3:20, "Look! I stand at the door and knock. If you hear my voice and open the door, I will come in, and we will share a meal together as friends. Those who are victorious will sit with me on my throne, just as I was victorious and sat with my Father on his throne."

CHAPTER 1

God's Selected

Num 1:2–4, "And the Lord spoke to Moses while still at Mt. Sinai," From the whole community of Israel, record the names of all the warriors by their clans and families. List all the men twenty years old or older who are able to go to war. You and Aaron must register the troops, and you will be assisted by one family leader from each tribe."

In this beautiful and timeless book, we're going to see the importance of the very first census—a cross-examination of men who are eligible, able, and ready to serve and go to battle for the Lord. Taking a census was a long and tedious task, but this was a vital assignment to ensure the quality of Israel's military strength before they entered the Promise Land.

In this journey, we will see God bridging the gap on who is willing and ready to serve Him—and then watch His purpose and plans unfold. We will see how God can prepare His people even when they continue to rebel. God's plans were organized at the beginning but then became disorganized (because of the Israelite's ignorance), and finally were reorganized and back on track. Doesn't this apply to many of us today?

God placed His children in those circumstances in the wilderness for a reason. It should have developed an inner strength of Whom to lean on and go to for everything. But as we will see in this journey, that would not be the case in so many instances. Just like our times in the wilderness today, His children needed to know who they were as His chosen ones—and to not trust in themselves but in Almighty God.

When God's children were in bondage in Egypt, they were just a number to the evil rulers. Now they're a number "with a name" in the eyes of God, set forth on a journey for the next thirty-eight-plus years to the Promise Land! All they have to do is to be willing and allow God to lead them in all His ways, with no excuses. This chapter shows how God can select various people to fulfill His plan in life's journey!

The Old Testament focuses on Israel as God's chosen people. In Deut 7:7–9, Moses tells the children of Israel why God chose them: "The Lord did not set his affection on you and choose you because you were more numerous than other people, for you were the fewest of all. But it was because the Lord loved you and would show His faithfulness in keeping His oath. He swore to your ancestors that he brought you out with a mighty hand and redeemed you from the land of slavery, from the power of Pharaoh, king of Egypt. Know therefore that the Lord your God is God; he is the faithful God, keeping his covenant of love to a thousand generations of those who love him and keep his commandments." Once again, we see that God's choice is not based on the merit of a particular person or nation but solely on His love and faithfulness—because God is always true to His word, as we will see.[1]

When God chooses us for any task, it should be an incredible privilege, honor, and blessing—because He has given you and me unique gifts and a special calling to serve Him and His people in some shape or form. You may be asked to lead a church, teach Sunday school, counsel someone, mentor someone weaker in faith, serve in the community, or provide spiritual guidance to someone who is in their lowest time of life.

There are so many opportunities of service for every one of God's children. We must instill the following passages in our hearts and minds daily. God's word reminds us in John 15:16 when Jesus says, "You did not choose me, but I chose you and appointed you so that you might go and bear fruit—fruit that will last—and so that whatever you ask in my name the Father will give you." Eph 1:4 says, "He chose us in him before the creation of the world to be holy and blameless in his sight." And 1 Pet 2:9 says, "You are a chosen people, a royal priesthood, a holy nation, God's special possession, that you may declare the praises of him who called you out of darkness into his wonderful light."

Today so many Christians don't see their own abilities in how they can serve our Lord & Savior in great and mighty ways. Maybe it's because "they don't see what God's power can do through them"—and that eye-opener could make all the difference. After all, this is the Almighty God, the One Who can heal and save us. He is Omnipotent, Omniscient, and Omni-Present and hears our cries and knows our every need. He provides us with an abundance of blessings, created us in His image, and gave us eternal life by faith through His Son, Jesus Christ. This is the Sovereign God who chose you and me and can do

1. "Why Did God Choose Me?"

anything He wants! We just need to lean upon Him and trust in all His ways, and He will guide us as faithful servants.

Peter reminds us in his second epistle that God has given us everything we need to live a life that honors Him. So, what is the root cause of our unwillingness to surrender our services to Him? If there is no deficiency in His power, the lack must be in our faith. Don't we realize we're eligible because we're made in His image? He's our Father, and He loves us. We're not second-class people, we're first-class in His eyes, and He's ready to lead us down His path, and there should be no excuses.

However, today the enemy is on a fiery trail conducting his battles in our minds and disabling many to feel they're not included in God's family or even a part of His plan, which keeps us from excellent service. Isa 45:18 reminds us," For the LORD is God, and He created the heavens and Earth and put everything in place. He made the world to be lived in (by us), not to be a place of empty chaos. "I am the LORD," He says, "and there is no other," and in Num 14:21, *"But as truly as I live, all the Earth shall be filled with the glory of the LORD."*

As we can see, you and I are part of God's Master Plan. Together we provide the vehicle through which God will fill the Earth with His glory, and we can genuinely reveal the glory of the LORD because we're an inclusive group that is part of His family and grand plan. When we're abiding in Him, we're set apart from others to accomplish His task, revealing the character of Christ in our everyday life and preparing to dwell with Him in a land forever!

1 Cor 1:26–31, "Remember, dear brothers and sisters, that few of you were wise in the world's eyes or powerful or wealthy when God called you. Instead, God chose things the world considers foolish in order to shame those who think they are wise. And he chose things that are powerless to shame those who are powerful. God chose things despised by the world, things counted as nothing at all, and used them to bring to nothing what the world considers important. As a result, no one can ever boast in the presence of God. God has united you with Christ Jesus. For our benefit, God made him to be wisdom itself. Christ made us right with God; he made us pure and holy, and he freed us from sin. Therefore, as the Scriptures say, "If you want to boast, boast only about the LORD."

He selected you and me to glorify Him through our works of faithful service for His Kingdom—while boasting about what He is doing in and through us. This is not the same earthly boast of selfish pride but boasting of God's great attributes—showing the world what He has done for us as believers, what He is still doing, and what He has promised to do in the future!

CHAPTER 2

God's Organization

Num 2:1–2, "Then the Lord gave these instructions to Moses and Aaron: "When the Israelites set up camp, each tribe will be assigned "its own" area. The tribal divisions will camp beneath their family banners on all four sides of the Tabernacle but at some distance from it."

God's children have now been on this Exodus journey for over a year, and during this time, their assembly amongst the people was not very structured, with no discipline. But now, they were getting ready to go into the land God had promised, so they needed organization amongst the nation. You must love this chapter because this type of Godly order has some striking parallels to God's creation in Genesis chapter one.

When God created the heavens and the earth and all that filled it with His order of glory, beauty, purpose, and amazement—He also calls on His people to form themselves under His guidelines with a disposition of splendor, meaning, wonder, and honor. This was so important because we're representing His orderly plans on earth.

Israel was organized by tribe for various reasons; it was an effective way to manage & govern large groups of people and simplified the division of the Promise Land. Plus, it was part of their culture & heritage. It was easier to keep track of their genealogies because this was the only way to prove they were part of God's chosen people and nation. Finally, it made traveling so much more productive & efficient.

You talk about inner circles; each tribe followed its standard, for they were melting pots within their own clan. I am sure if you brought them all together, there would be chaos and confusion because there was a difference in their culture! This reminds me of a few cliquish areas I've lived in throughout my life. Some were very territorial within their own society, culture, and lifestyle. Their body language and choice of words clarified that there was no common ground or way of connecting to their little world. How foolish! They need to watch the Andy Griffith episode I mentioned earlier in the book.

When you read this short verse and summary, you will see the importance of organization in accomplishing God's plan. God is simply a God of structure—look at His wondrous universe in all its splendor and how it functions; it is mind-blowing! When there is no organization or discipline, what happens? Chaos, confusion, division, and dissension lead to only one thing: a total breakdown of the initial plan. God is a God of complete order because this attribute is essential to His divine character.

Within His very being, the Lord is orderly and is always consistent. Since our God is a God of order, we should be, too. We were created to think with reason, discernment, and consider all aspects of a matter. And when we need help in any given circumstance, especially when we feel things are about to fall apart, our Great and Almighty God invites us to "come, let us reason together" (Isa 1:18).

A recent Gallup organization and the National Opinion Research Center study revealed that 78 percent of all Americans claim they want to experience some form of spiritual growth. Half of this group felt they were too busy with their careers to enjoy God or even give enough time to develop their spiritual lives. Apparently, the people polled in this survey had no spiritual structure or discipline in their daily life.

But here's the critical takeaway! When these people were polled about their workplace, it was found that when businesses provided spiritually-minded programs, they felt not only calmer and more relaxed but were, in fact, more productive.[1] The key to this type of progression is simple, Christ-centered living rooted in genuine integrity and commitment!

God's word reminds us in 1 Cor 14:33, "For God is not a God of disorder but of peace, as in all the meetings of God's holy people." It's so critical for God's children to remember that when we're in times of worship or service for Him, our actions will either demonstrate one of order or disorder (Spirit or the flesh). A Christian enabling the gifts of the Holy Spirit—exercised to their fullest—is portraying the Fruit of the Spirit and our Lord at its best. This illustration is a clear monitor on someone filled with the work of the Spirit—because if they are not a peacemaker and embodying God's work, it's all about them and their agenda, not God.

---

1. "What Principles Should Distinguish a Christian Business?"

When we, as God's children, wonder why the Holy Spirit is not moving in some churches and communities, it's this: God cannot work when there's no Godly order because He's not a God of confusion and chaos but one of peace, love, order, and organization under His guidelines, not humans!

1 Cor 14:40, "But be sure everything is done properly and in order."

Ps 37:23–24, "The LORD directs the steps of the godly. He delights in every detail of their lives. Though they stumble, they will never fall, for the LORD holds them by the hand."

CHAPTER 3

God's Appointed

Num 3:11–13, "Then the LORD spoke to Moses, saying: "Now behold, I Myself have taken the Levites from among the children of Israel instead of every firstborn who opens the womb among the children of Israel. Therefore, the Levites shall be Mine (wow) because all the firstborn *are* Mine. On the day that I struck all the firstborn in the land of Egypt, I sanctified to Myself all the firstborn in Israel, both man and beast. They shall be Mine: I *am* the LORD."

This is a powerful statement from God on the position of the Levites, for they were set apart for specific roles of service. God highly appointed them, and He had His stamp of approval on this select group! The profoundness of this passage is that God had a preference" They were His ideal choice!"

The Levites had proved themselves to be the most suitable of all the tribes for God through their firm and faithful defense of the honor of the Lord at the worship of the golden calf (Ex 32:26). They did not cave into the pagan practices for they knew their obligation was to the Almighty One alone!

What set the Levites apart from the other tribes? Why were they God's ideal choice? First, God chose them because they obeyed Him, and then God promised to provide for the Levites from the abundance of all the other tribes (Num 18:8–14). Second, because of their godly position, the Levites were appointed priests with sacred duties, unlike the other tribes. And with this responsibility, they were held to the most stringent standards of behavior and ritual purity (Lev chapter 21). Third, they had to be twenty-five years of age before they could enter service, which illustrates they were mature before they would go into training. This is vital because, based on some research and bible commentators, they probably received at least five years of on-the-job training before they were admitted entirely to full-time service at thirty. Then, they were ready for service as God's appointed because they were equipped, skilled, and, most importantly, had God's support!

One of the most familiar passages in the Old Testament is recorded in Jeremiah 1:5, where God's word says, "The Lord gave me a message, He said. I knew you before I formed you in your mother's womb. Before you were born, I set you apart and appointed you as My spokesman to the world." God reminds us and assures us that He has a purpose for every Christian, but some of us are called and appointed for specific types of work.

So many examples are laid out in God's word on how He used various men and women to fulfill His will. This is a short list, but Noah, Moses, Abraham and the Patriarchs, Joshua, Samson, David, Solomon, Daniel, Ezekiel, Isaiah, Jeremiah, Jonah, Rahab, Ruth, Esther, John the Baptist, Paul, Peter, John, and other Disciples.

As His chosen ones, when we come to the complete understanding, knowledge, and wisdom that God made us and saved us (through His Son) for a reason and purpose, we will see that we're laid under further obligations to serve Him faithfully. This is important because we're His ideal choice for service today!

We must realize God has "full rights of service through each one of us" because of the price He paid for you and me through the sacrifice of Jesus Christ, His Son. This confirms the right He has as our Father and Creator. After all, He created us in His image and expects us to exemplify His divine characteristics! While He doesn't force us, as His chosen ones, we should feel obligated to serve Him in ways that "show our stamp of His approval and our appointed role of service in this life" Rom 13:13–14.

We're not here to live out a life of complacency and comfort, but we're called and chosen to grow and serve in ways for the glory of the Lord (Phil 1:11). If we do not know what that task is, then we need to seek and discover that common ground of Christlike wisdom and obedience from His word— empowered by the Holy Spirit so we can attain clear guidance. He will make it known in His timing so we will know why, what, where, when, and how to serve. Don't be concerned about weaknesses, fears, anxieties, and failures. He will always provide us with all the resources to accomplish His job (2 Pet 1:3–11), and He reassures us that He will be with us until its completion (Phil 1:6).

As Christ's church, you and I are a "royal priesthood" declaring honor and praise to God in everything we say and do. This highly esteemed and distinct title appoints us to offer sacrifices that are pleasing to God while representing Him to the world; this should be considered both a privilege and a responsibility.

God's word reminds us in 1 Pet 2:9, "But you are not like that, for you are a chosen people. You are royal priests, a holy nation, God's very own possession. As a result, you can show others the goodness of God, for he called you out of the darkness into his wonderful light."

While Peter addresses Jewish believers specifically in this passage, we discover that Christ-followers will one day participate in God's kingdom. Today, as followers of Christ, we serve as a kind of royal priesthood and as His appointed Citizens of Heaven on earth proclaiming God's excellencies. What a high-calling and distinct honor. But in the near future, we will indeed be God's citizens of a kingdom that will one day come to Earth (see Col 3:1–4)[1].

> Heb 5:1–15, "Every high priest is a man chosen to represent other people in their dealings with God. He presents their gifts to God and offers sacrifices for their sins. And he is able to deal gently with ignorant and wayward people because he himself is subject to the same weaknesses. That is why he must offer sacrifices for his own sins as well as theirs. And no one can become a high priest simply because he wants such an honor. He must be called by God for this work, just as Aaron was. That is why Christ did not honor himself by assuming he could become High Priest. No, he was chosen by God, who said to him, "You are my Son. Today I have become your Father."

---

1. "What Does it Mean that We Are a Royal Priesthood?"

CHAPTER 4

God's Elite

Num 4:1–5," Then the LORD said to Moses and Aaron, "Record the names of the members of the clans and families of the Kohathite division of the tribe of Levi. List all the men between the ages of thirty and fifty who are eligible to serve in the Tabernacle. The duties of the Kohathites at the Tabernacle will relate to the most sacred objects. When the camp moves, Aaron and his sons must enter the Tabernacle first to take down the inner curtain and cover the Ark of the Covenant with it."

The Kohathites were one of three divisions part of the Levite tribe. Kohath is dealt with before Gershon and is given an esteemed duty: transporting the holiest furnishings of the Tabernacle. The reason for this elevation of the second son over his older brother is based on the sovereign selection of the Lord. But also the favored work He gives this family as it relates to the holiest things of God. This is a classic example that God can elevate the unexpected and show favor to whomever He chooses.

In the culture of the Old Testament, an elder son was always favored over a younger son. But that is not always so with God. He can do the unexpected to anyone He chooses to show favor to. Especially those who have a crucial role in taking out their responsibility in "every detail for the Lord"—for they are an elite group—whom God has appointed.

Paul reminds us in Rom 9:18–23, "So you see, God chooses to show mercy to some, and he chooses to harden the hearts of others, so they refuse to listen. Well then, you might say, "Why does God blame people for not responding? Haven't they simply done what he makes them do?"

No, don't say that. Who are you, a mere human being, to argue with God? Should the thing that was created say to the one who created it, "Why have you made me like this?"

When a potter makes jars out of clay, doesn't he have a right to use the same lump of clay to make one jar for decoration and another to throw garbage into? In the same way, even though God has the right to show his anger and his power, he is very patient with those on whom his anger falls, who are destined for destruction. He does this to make the riches of his glory shine even brighter on those to whom he shows mercy, who were prepared in advance for glory."

Paul is not conveying to us that some people are worth more than others, but the ultimate decision is made by our Heavenly Creator—Who controls all created things. We have no right to demand specific things from God because everything depends on Him—and His choosing by His will. God reminds us in Isaiah chapter fifty-five that His ways and thoughts are above ours, for He is the Almighty and Sovereign God, who knows all. If we believe in His choosing for all things, we will less likely allow our selfish pride to creep in. The most important thing we must remember regarding God's selection process is that His name and power will be glorified in one way or another!

Who would not want to play a vital role in God's plan and bring glory and honor to His name, such as this group of Levites? Because the same God who calls out the stars by their name will leave nothing unarranged in His service, for "He knows who wants to be a part of His plan." Yes, it requires preparation and training to be part of His team—just like the rigorous training the Kohathites had to undergo to carry out this most critical task for God.

The job description in this chapter shows us that a Levite must be between the ages of thirty and fifty. They were expected to carry out these duties and responsibilities in every detail prescribed by God. If not, their failure to do so could result in death. So, what is God telling us here as an example for us today?

Worshipping, praising, and serving a Holy God must be taken seriously because it's part of our Christlike DNA as believers. It's not a once-a-week default button; it's part of our daily life and a high calling. It's not just a reaction but a response to our Lord in every aspect of our lives. This is one area of measurement where quantity and quality play out our genuine commitment to God! We should be in His presence and company daily, ready and prepared at His disposal if we're part of His elite group. Why?

Because we're God's management company on earth, and as His establishment, we're His best picks of the crop. We're his elect, first and upper class, and A-List. Our central role is to be effective stewards of His detailed plan!

We have a managerial responsibility encompassed in two key areas: 1) Preserve the Holiness of God (set ourselves apart & stay spiritually grounded), and 2) Expand His Righteousness (Christlike attributes displayed in our lives—ongoing).

When we set forth to achieve these tasks, we stay connected with God. He shows favor to the ones who delight in, connect with, and give honor to Him. Isa 66:2 says, "These are the ones I look on with favor: those who are humble and contrite in spirit, and who tremble at my word." When we have the favor of the Lord, we rest in quiet confidence that we're forgiven (Rom 4:7), we are within the plan of God (Ps 86:11), and that He is always there for us (Isa 41:10; Matt 28:20).

When we're in that place of knowing God is with us, we feel connected to His Almighty power through His Spirit. And it is then we obtain His understanding to live as His elite according to His will while promoting godliness in every part of our life. We must live as active Christians so we will not fall easy prey to the temptations of this world. As believers, we feel His favor in our spirit when we're in the zone of Christlikeness. And in that close walk, we begin to see and appreciate every little blessing God provides for our enjoyment—and we no longer take them for granted.

Remember, God will seek out those who love Him and His commands so that He can bless, guide, and protect them (Psalm 37:23; Proverbs 3:5–6). This does not mean we will not experience difficult stages in our life. But as His children, we will know that God is with us through it all.

Those who possess the favor of God know that He is with them and nothing can happen apart from His good purpose and plan (Romans 8:28). They lend their ear to His quiet and calm voice as they walk through the dark valleys (Psalm 34:15) and know that their struggle to "remain faithful to Him will not go unrewarded" (Matthew 10:42; Revelation 2:10). And that is the greatest blessing of all![1]

> Tit 2:12–15, "And we are instructed to turn from godless living and sinful pleasures. We should live in this evil world with wisdom, righteousness, and devotion to God while we look forward with hope to that wonderful day when the glory of our great God and Savior, Jesus Christ, will be revealed. He gave his life to free us from every kind of sin, to cleanse us, and to make us his very own people, totally committed to doing good deeds. You must teach these things and encourage the believers to do them. You have the authority to correct them when necessary, so don't let anyone disregard what you say."

1. "What is the Favor of God, and How Can I Get it?"

CHAPTER 5

God's Purified

Num 5:1–3," The LORD gave these instructions to Moses: "Command the people of Israel to remove from the camp anyone who has a skin disease or a discharge, or who has become ceremonially unclean by touching a dead person. This command applies to men and women alike. Remove them so they will not defile the camp in which I live among them."

As Israel was preparing to march to the Promise Land, they must separate themselves from those considered to be ceremonially unclean. These three sources were reminders of the effects of sin and an analogy of humanity's sinful nature inherited from Adam.

At this stage in Israel's progression to the Promise Land, they had been organized and ordered by God, and now they would be challenged to become a community that "valued purity" in their lives. God desired to make Israel a "Promised Land people," which meant a purified and holy people dedicated to God alone! They now represent Him and not a pagan nation of impurities![1]

The main issue in the laws of purity in the nation of Israel was not magic, health, or superstition; the great reality was the presence of a Holy and Pure God in the camp, and there could be no uncleanness where he dwells. God is concerned with far more than our individual acts of sin; He demands that our sinful nature be addressed. Only in Jesus can our sinful nature— (the old man) be crucified, and the nature of Jesus (the new man) be given to us, making us new creations. *"God does not have a relationship of love and fellowship with the old man, but He does with the new man."*

1. "Numbers 5—Separating from Sin."

Since we were created in the image of God—and we're to be His imitators (Eph 5:1), we must pursue a purified life as devoted children of our Heavenly Creator. Living pure and clean lives should be our daily goal—not only in the sight of God but as His representatives on this earth, as His witnesses, in every facet of our life. It should include our conduct, words, thoughts, service, worship, and fellowship.

Galatians chapter five reminds us that those controlled by their sinful desires will produce vices that could never be part of a Holy God. But if we live by the power of God's Spirit, what flows from our lives are by-products that will portray holy cleanliness and purity. Always remember that to be pure and holy, we must be declared righteous, set apart for His good use, and we all know who our model of Righteousness is (1 Cor 1:30).

It is so easy for us all to fall prey to our flesh, for there is so much impurity, falsehood, unloving, unforgiving, unholy, unrighteous, and unclean ways consuming our lives in this society and culture today. God even teaches us "His value of cleanness" through His creation—because He created natural cycles that keep our air and water clean that help us to sustain ourselves in daily life. God's word tells us in Jer 10:12, "But the LORD made the earth by his power, and he preserves it by his wisdom. With his own understanding, he stretched out the heavens."

Think of how the earth cleans itself, even after humans have polluted it. Does this happen by chance or by the design of an Almighty Creator? Rom 1:20 tells us, "For ever since the world was created, people have seen the earth and sky. Through everything God made, they can clearly see his invisible qualities—his eternal power and divine nature. So, they have no excuse for not knowing God." This passage reveals God's divine nature of might, intelligence, and intricate detail of His creation. It shows us that He controls powerful resources for our good to sustain us, but He also expects us to be good stewards of His purity.

Purity is freedom from anything that contaminates or can pollute our daily lives. God desires we live purely in all our dealings (Ezek 45:10; Luke 6:31). As stated earlier; purity should define our thought life (2 Cor 10:5), our words (Eph 4:29), and our actions (1 Cor 10:31). Jesus said, "Blessed are the pure in heart, for they shall see God" (Matt 5:8).

When our hearts are clouded with impurities, we cannot experience God's presence. As we draw nearer to God and come to know Him more, His desires will naturally become ours. The opposite of purity is "impurity," and the prefix "im" means "not." When you break this down, those living a life of impurity "is not" allowing the Lord to create His cleanness in their life. When we've tasted the Lord's goodness, our desire to live a pure life is more apparent with each passing day (Ps 34:8).

Genuine believers in Jesus Christ experience the tastes of God's goodness and grace when they; 1) Observe the beauty of His creation and recognize His blessings and care, 2) Take high regard for His holiness and infinite righteousness, 3) Appreciate the cost of Christ's sacrifice for our salvation, 4) Trust God and seek Him as our sole source for all things, 5) Recognize His answered prayers in our life, 6) Acknowledge the truth of His word and promises, and 7) Realize He left us with a Helper, Counselor, and Comforter to get us through the most challenging stages of life. The only way to genuinely taste and see that the Lord is good is to put the matter to the test because when you look at this list in all His ways, you will come to know that God is good all the time.

When we come to grips with the bloodshed that Christ poured out on the cross, which washed away the filthiness of our lives and made our sins as white as snow— maybe we can get a holy glimpse of the sincerity and severity of just how much it means to God when we strive to live a life of purity and cleanness! Letting that sink into our hearts, soul, and minds could make a massive difference in how we see the importance of Christlike purity.

> Isa 1:18–20, "Come now, let's settle this," says the LORD. "Though your sins are like scarlet, I will make them as white as snow. Though they are red like crimson, I will make them as white as wool. If you will only obey me, you will have plenty to eat, but if you turn away and refuse to listen, you will be devoured by the sword of your enemies. I, the LORD, have spoken!"

Just a thought. If personal hygiene and spiritual purity are intricately linked in the Bible, this is a powerful and striking depiction of the importance of our Christian life, "internally and externally."

CHAPTER 6

God's Way

Num 6:1–4, "Then the LORD said to Moses, "Give the following in-structions to the people of Israel. "If any of the people, either men or women, take the special vow of a Nazirite, setting themselves apart to the LORD in a special way, they must give up wine and other alcoholic drinks. They must not use vinegar made from wine or from other alcoholic drinks, they must not drink fresh grape juice, and they must not eat grapes or raisins. As long as they are bound by their Nazirite vow, they are not allowed to eat or drink anything that comes from a grapevine—not even the grape seeds or skins."

In the day of Moses', a personal vow was as binding as a written contract or agreement. Why? Because this type of personal commitment is considered more serious when you solemnly vow to do it! God instituted the Nazirite vow for a reason; it was set aside for people who wanted to devote time entirely only to serving God. The vow was a decision, action, and desire for the person whose aim and willingness to yield themselves entirely to God.

It was a voluntary commitment, and it included three well-defined restrictions: 1) One must abstain from wine and any fermented drink, 2) The person's hair could not be cut and the beard could not be shaved, and 3) Touching a dead body was prohibited. This specific vow and commitment aimed to raise up a group of leaders who would be devout to God's ways.

This was a special dedication with the idea of something exceptional and extraordinary, significantly beyond a normal promise. This was a comprehensive vow concerning what one ate, how one looked, and with whom one associated. The Nazirites vowed to express one's craving and longing to draw close to God—and separate themselves from the world's comforts and pleasures.

There were several remarkable Nazirites in the Bible: Samson, John the Baptist, and Paul—this is an excellent company to be in. The Nazirites were forbidden to eat or drink anything from the grapevine; this was a form of self-denial connected with the idea of a special consecration to God—dedicated to a divine purpose!

There is no greater expression of oneself when they desire to draw closer to the Lord by denying their natural will and instead following His will and plan. It does not mean we ignore our likes and dislikes in life; it means we pursue spiritual choices and not our natural, human interests that can separate us from the will of God. Our focus and commitment should always be nestled in obedience to God's will.

One key evidence of our consecrated life in the Lord is when we walk by the power of His Spirit, apply His word in our lives, have a vibrant prayer life, develop Christlikeness, and help build others up. We will have a constant battle with the enemy, but in a "wholehearted dedication" to the Lord, our capacity to follow and commit to the Spirit will grow more and more each day (Gal 5:24).

One of the great Nazirites, Paul, tells us in Romans chapter twelve how to behave, be personally responsible as Christians, and offer our bodies as a living sacrifice to God. What does this mean? Our very lives as His creation are intended to bring glory and honor to God because we are made in His image and share His divine characteristics. But it's all in how we handle those beautiful attributes daily.

He desires us to lay aside our selfish desires, forget our own agenda, pick up our cross daily, and follow Him. When we apply all our energy, time, and resources to His use and trust Him to guide us through our life journey, the world will see the evidence of our acts and ways of godliness.

These steps of progression are essential. Why? Because it exemplifies our gratitude, love, and obedience from a genuine Christlike heart. Always remember that God has a good, pleasing, and perfect plan for those who love Him and are called according to His purpose. He wants the best for us; however, He wants us to be transformed with renewed minds living in a manner of obedience and love that honors Him.

We can only do this when we're not copying the behaviors of this world, and we willingly and humbly submit ourselves to Him for His use. While the world only offers a life of selfishness, and unholy and corruptible deeds, when we commit our ways to the ways of His word, with the guidance of the Holy Spirit, we see a life exhibiting selflessness, holiness, and righteousness. Our flesh is weak, and it's so easy to succumb to the values and ways of the world.

That's why we must dive deep into the richness, fullness, and breadth of God's word and firmly plant and root His ways into our minds and heart.

Even in our all-out attempts to steer away from the practices of this wicked world, we can still be blindsided by the enemy's tricks of covetousness, foolishness, stubbornness, and ignorance. When we are found grounded in the word of God and allowing the Holy Spirit to refresh, renew, and redirect our paths, we can be changed and used for such a divine purpose that God has in store for you and me. God's unique ways require a determined focus.

A loyal follower of Jesus Christ knows that living a life of godliness lies in this: Their life, hope, and truth are grounded in their love, obedience, and faith in the One who will help them overcome, endure, persevere, manage, and portray a life that is honoring Him! They realize the potential to fulfill a satisfying and gratifying life with a purpose and cause that is second to none. When our hearts and minds are transformed to Christlikeness, we are more adept at recognizing our errors in life, thinking biblically, behaving obediently, acting lovingly, living peacefully, conveying words gracefully, extending more mercy, and building lives fruitfully—for there is truly no other way.

> Deut 5:32–33, "So Moses told the people, "You must be careful to obey all the commands of the LORD your God, following his instructions in every detail. Stay on the path that the LORD your God has commanded you to follow. Then you will live long and prosperous lives in the land you are about to enter and occupy."

CHAPTER 7

Godly Distribution

Num 7:2–5, "Then the leaders of Israel—the tribal leaders who had registered the troops—came and brought their offerings. Together they brought six large wagons and twelve oxen. There was a wagon for every two leaders and an ox for each leader. They presented these to the LORD in front of the Tabernacle. Then the LORD said to Moses, "Receive their gifts and use these oxen and wagons for transporting the Tabernacle. Distribute them among the Levites according to the work they have to do.""

In this passage, we see the importance of how these items were offered before the LORD and the Tabernacle, which emphasizes the holy aspect of their offering. They were given to God and then assigned to meet the needs of others. We also see a beautiful depiction of organization, unity, willingness, integrity, and accountability.

The leaders of each tribe bring six carts (a cart for every two of the leaders) and twelve oxen (each one an ox) given to transport the Tabernacle through the wilderness. All twelve tribes brought gifts and offerings for its use and maintenance. After all, it was everyone's Tabernacle, so they all participated in this together! But we also see a powerful undertone of distribution—the most to those with the heaviest burdens to bear.

Throughout scripture, we see passages on how God has blessed us with gifts, talents, and possessions—but also His expectations from His children in what we do with those blessings. Are we handling them in a way that honors Him? Examples: 1) Utilize our God-given gifts and talents to build up His church and help others (1 Pet 4:10–11 1 Cor 12:14), 2) Put to use our knowledge of God's word in encouraging and edifying the body of Christ (2

Tim 3:16–17), and 3) Use the financial blessings in our lives for the storing of treasures in Heaven, not on earth (Matt 6:19–21, 2 Cor 9:6–9).

In the first parable recorded in Matt 13:10–13, we see the very familiar passage that says, "His disciples came and asked him, "Why do you use parables when you talk to the people?" He replied, "You are permitted to understand the secrets of the Kingdom of Heaven, but others are not. To those who listen to my teaching, more understanding will be given, and they will have an abundance of knowledge. But for those who are not listening, even what little understanding they have will be taken away from them. That is why I use these parables, for they look, but they don't really see. They hear, but they don't really listen or understand."

In the heart of this passage, Jesus reminds us that we're all responsible for effectively using what we have. If we enjoy blessings from God as His true children, how much more joy can we experience if we distribute them proportionately to others in need? This could be from a physical, emotional, or, most importantly, spiritual sense.

I love this powerful devotion from Charles Stanley. God's word reminds us in 2 Cor 9:6–9, "Remember this—a farmer who plants only a few seeds will get a small crop. But the one who plants generously will get a generous crop. You must each decide in your heart how much to give. And don't give reluctantly or in response to pressure. "For God loves a person who gives cheerfully." And God will generously provide all you need. Then you will always have everything you need and plenty left over to share with others."

As the Scriptures say, "They share freely and give generously to the poor. Their good deeds will be remembered forever." God's blessings to us are not meant to end with us. He desires them to flow to others. This principle applies in all areas of life, including finances. Did you know that our heavenly Father has plans for your money? The Lord graciously provides for our needs and even our wants. But He also wants us to use our money to achieve His plans. And one of His goals is that we share our resources with others. Just look at His extravagant promise in verse 8 of today's passage: "And God is able to make all grace overflow to you, so that, always having all sufficiency in everything, you may have an abundance for every good deed."

Sharing blessings with others will never lead to deprivation. In fact, the Lord promises to increase the harvest of our righteousness and enrich us in everything in response to our generosity. We can never outgive God. A hoarded blessing won't ever be enjoyed as richly as a shared one. Using your gift to meet someone else's needs glorifies God by demonstrating His grace at work in your life. Don't let His generous provisions end with you. Pass them on and discover the joy of a never-ending cycle of blessings.[1]

At the heart of sharing God's goodness with others is rooted in genuine care for all of God's creation. An ambassador of Christ will not make it a habit of selfishness but one of selflessness because they want others to experience God's blessings. I read a secular article on the practice, principles, importance, qualifications, and compliance of sound distribution. Laid out in this illustration are PowerPoints we can use in our Christian lives today. "Good distribution practice is a set of standards for sourcing, handling, storing, and transporting goods with quality, safety, and security. Good distribution practice is vital because it dramatically affects public health."

"Any mistake in distribution can cause shortages, delays, and even the introduction of falsified goods! Overall, following good distribution practices protects distributors from situations that would not only damage their reputation in the industry but also harm the general public and lead to a massive loss of customers. If the goods are not adequately secured or distributed, it can result in serious injuries, property damage, and even fatalities."[2]

This is a powerful rule of thumb to follow as a daily guide—because the improper and misleading distribution of God's word can lead to disastrous outcomes. So, if we don't use our God-given abilities to spread His Good News "properly and truthfully," it will lead to spiritual casualties.

Do we realize as followers and distributors of the Gospel that God has given us all the resources we need (2 Peter 1:3)? The power of His word and Spirit is our source. It's our responsibility to transmit this information to everyone within our proximity. It's vital in how we store His words in our minds and hearts so it can be presented and shared with others in good standing. It should be done with quality (from a genuine heart) for the well-being of all people who want to receive it, accept it, and use it as well.

If we lack the proper distribution of what God has given us, it can lead to our shortfall in blessings for not just you and me but that one person who needs it the most! Following God's guidelines of proper distribution protects you and all recipients; it's for our good! Productive and effective allocation of God's message to the world hinges on this one primary ingredient, unity! The goods will never reach their ultimate destination without everyone on the same path. Being united as one is what the Lord expects from His body of believers. Why?

Because the church is His body, and we "should" all move together in unison but only at the direction of the Head of the Church, and that is Jesus

---

1. Stanley, "Blessed to Bless Others."
2. Francisco, "A Guide to Good Distribution."

Christ (Col 1:18). Since Jesus is the Head, He expects His body to cooperate in peace, harmony, and love, always remembering that His love binds us together! Utilizing all our gifts as one with the same goal in mind and at heart is a key to unity.

Phil 2:3 reminds us, "Don't be selfish; don't try to impress others. Be humble, thinking of others as better than yourselves. Don't look out only for your own interests, but take an interest in others, too. You must have the same attitude that Christ Jesus had." If we don't have the same attitude as Christ, there will never be unity in His body of believers.

Disunity in a church is often caused when we act selfishly and consider ourselves better than others. Most importantly, as Christians, we are to see one another in the light of the cross! A church full of such people enjoying their "common salvation in Christ" is the sign of a true, biblical church unified in Jesus, participating in love and grace, distributing, and reciprocating godly blessings; accordingly. This type of mindset and heart is needed in churches today!

> Luke 6:37–38, "Do not judge others, and you will not be judged. Do not condemn others, or it will all come back against you. Forgive others, and you will be forgiven. Give, and you will receive. Your gift will return to you in full, pressed down, shaken together to make room for more, running over, and poured into your lap. The amount you give will determine the amount you get back."

> Luke 12:47–48, "And a servant who knows what the master wants, but isn't prepared and doesn't carry out those instructions, will be severely punished. But someone who does not know, and then does something wrong, will be punished only lightly. When someone has been given much, much will be required in return; and when someone has been entrusted with much, even more will be required."

CHAPTER 8

God's Lampstand

Num 8:1–4, "The LORD said to Moses, "Give Aaron the following instructions: When you set up the seven lamps in the lampstand, place them so their light shines forward in front of the
lampstand." So, Aaron did this. He set up the seven lamps so they
reflected their light forward, just as the LORD had commanded
Moses. The entire lampstand, from its base to its decorative blos-
soms, was made of beaten gold. It was built according to the exact
design the LORD had shown Moses."

The purpose of the lampstand was not to make light "but to make it more visible." The lamps burned specially made olive oil and needed to be continually
filled to provide constant light. "A lamp without oil that is not burning is useless" because they provided light for the priests as they carried out their daily
duties. This was needed because they could not perform their tasks without
light. But another powerful point of this constant light is this; it portrays God's
presence.

The light from the lampstand in the Tabernacle was focused on bringing
the most illumination to the rest of the tent—like we are to the rest of the
world. This is important because the lampstand symbolizes the church—and
today, we are the church! And to carry this illustration further, oil is widely
understood as the symbol of the Holy Spirit. So, without the oil (Holy Spirit)
working in us, we are useless and not burning Christ's light in a darkened
world.

The lampstand was to be made of pure gold, hammered out to the perfect accuracy of God's requirements. It was placed in the first section, called
the Holy Place (Heb 9:2), designed to give forth light day and night (Exod

27:20–21). It was the only source of light within the Tabernacle, the same type of Light that points directly to Christ as the Light of the world (John 8:12; 9:5).

One of the most beautiful scriptures in God's word that parallels this passage is the parable of the ten bridesmaids, as recorded in Matt 25:1–13, where it says, "Then the Kingdom of Heaven will be like ten bridesmaids who took their lamps and went to meet the bridegroom. Five of them were foolish, and five were wise. The five who were foolish didn't take enough olive oil for their lamps, but the other five were wise enough to take along extra oil. When the bridegroom was delayed, they all became drowsy and fell asleep. "At midnight, they were roused by the shout, 'Look, the bridegroom is coming! Come out and meet him!' "All the bridesmaids got up and prepared their lamps. Then the five foolish ones asked the others, 'Please give us some of your oil because our lamps are going out.'

"But the others replied, 'We don't have enough for all of us. Go to a shop and buy some for yourselves.' "But while they were gone to buy oil, the bridegroom came. Then those who were ready went in with him to the marriage feast, and the door was locked. Later, when the other five bridesmaids returned, they stood outside, calling, 'Lord! Lord! Open the door for us!' "But he called back, 'Believe me; I don't know you!' "So, you, too, must keep watch! For you do not know the day or hour of my return."

In this powerful story, Jesus clearly details what it means to be ready and how we should live as dedicated Christians until He returns for you and me. In this parable, Christ is teaching us that every person is responsible and accountable for their own spiritual condition. So, the critical question is this. Are you dwelling in the darkness or His Light? Is your lampstand constantly full of His oil?

In this beautiful lesson, Jesus informs us to make sure our oil (Holy Spirit) is in use so His light can be seen in and through us—it must be in service every day, not periodically. Our spiritual preparation cannot be bought or borrowed because Christ is our only source; Jesus is the "true light that gives light to everyone" (John 1:9). This Light is only available based on our genuine relationship with Jesus Christ daily. We don't want to be caught in that moment of foolishness, and we find the door locked, and He says, "Believe me, I don't know you." If there was any fear of darkness or being left behind, it should be in this parable.

From the beginning, light has always dispelled darkness. However, when night falls, bad things seem to happen. While many of our enemies' dwell in the dark, we need the light to expose them—it's vital for our safety and security in everyday life. People need light because it elevates our focus on what is ahead of us, around us, and behind us. So, it should be when we enter our darkest times in life that we allow the use of that productive oil to go to work within us so we can turn on the light of Christ—so it's shining all the time.

I read an interesting comment from an atheist who once said, "However vast the darkness, we must supply our own light."[1] Consider the depths of these words from a person who does not believe in the eternal Light of the Living God. When our lives are so consumed by darkness, why can't Christians realize the source and power of the prevailing Light that can get us through all our darkest days? If we want to look or sound like the world, that will prevent us from sharing the source of Light in our life; we will succumb to the ways of our most woeful times. We're to illuminate His Light, not let it dim or fade away.

Below are some great quotes on darkness and light that can help motivate us in our darkest days. Isn't it amazing in all of God's providence how He can provide others with words of enlightenment that can impact other lives? While I don't agree with many of the below people's religious beliefs, their idioms of darkness and light are quite compelling.

- "Hope is being able to see that there is light despite all of the darkness." – Desmond Tutu

- "Even the darkest night will end, and the sun will rise." – Victor Hugo

- "Give light, and the darkness will disappear of itself." – Desiderius Erasmus

- "Maybe you have to know the darkness before you can appreciate the light." – Madeline L'Engle

- "In the midst of darkness, light persists." – Mahatma Gandhi

- "Darkness cannot drive out darkness: only light can do that. Hate cannot drive out hate: only love can do that." – Martin Luther King Jr.

- "We can easily forgive a child who is afraid of the dark; the real tragedy of life is when men are afraid of the light." – Plato

- "Why not dare yourself to become a shining positive light where darkness is the only thing known?" – Edmond Mbiaka

- "Look at how a single candle can both defy and define the darkness." – Anne Frank

- "You can't discover light by analyzing the dark." – Wayne Dyer

- "Peace and negativity cannot coexist just as light and darkness cannot coexist." – N. Goenka

1. Healy, "Quotes About Darkness and Light."

- "Life isn't just about darkness or light, rather it's about finding light within the darkness." – Landon Parham[2]

  "The Word gave life to everything that was created, and his life brought light to everyone. The light shines in the darkness, and the darkness can never extinguish it." John 1:4–5

2 Healy, "Quotes About Darkness and Light."

CHAPTER 9

Godly Motion

Num 9:17–19, "Whenever the cloud lifted from over the sacred tent, the people of Israel would break camp and follow it. And wherever the cloud settled, the people of Israel would set up camp. In this way, they traveled and camped at the Lord's command wherever he told them to go. Then they remained in their camp as long as the cloud stayed over the Tabernacle. If the cloud remained over the Tabernacle for a long time, the Israelites stayed and performed their duty to the Lord."

Even though God's children had been organized, cleansed, set apart, and blessed by Him, they still had to be guided by God each step, dependent upon Him alone to make it to the Promise Land. I love how this passage conveys that when the cloud moved (God), the people broke from their temporary camp and followed it until it settled wherever the Lord was, and they stayed there and served God until He moved again.

The cloud by day and the fire by night were help and support to the people of Israel. The fire at night was a comfort amidst a dark wilderness, and the cloud by day was a shade from the scorching sun in the wilderness. These were God's vehicles of presence and visible evidence of His moving, directing, protecting, and providing for His people through the wilderness.

What a beautiful depiction. Because through it all, every day—God's presence is with us. It's up to us if we want to camp with Him, but also be ready to pack up and fold our tents, hit the road again, and be in step with Him. We can't make a mistake and stick our selfish stakes too deep into our own ground—for if we do, it could prevent us from moving with God! If we cling too closely to our own personal surroundings, which are not of His will, it could be a sign that we do not depend on God 100%! But when we rely on our Lord wholeheartedly, it substantiates that our faith is steadfast in Him!

In Psalm chapter 124, God teaches us that we can depend on Him, and through all His protection and provisions, we will make it safely to the other side. In this passage, the Psalmist encourages us to affirm that we can and will persevere when God is with us. And when we know that beyond a shadow of a doubt, He's our game-changer. It will demonstrate Whom we depend upon, and no matter what, we will move when He leads us to move.

Depending on God is essential to the Christian life. We trust in or depend on God for our salvation (Eph 2:8–9). We rely on God for wisdom (Jas 1:5). In fact, we depend on God for everything (Ps 104:27) and in all life's circumstances (Prov 3:5–6). The Psalmist teaches the Lord's reliability with the three-fold description "The LORD is my rock, my fortress and my deliverer" (Ps 18:2).

We must always depend on God because we can do nothing in our own power. The Lord gives us the faith we need to make it through those times. Shadrach, Meshach, and Abednego couldn't sway the will of the king, and they couldn't lessen the intensity of the burning fiery furnace. They only knew that they could not bow down to a false god. So, they were thrown into the fire, depending on God alone for the outcome (Daniel chapter 3).

The key components lie in our prayer life. We honor our God by being a Doer of the Word, always abiding in Him, and not allowing worries, anxieties, and fears to overcome us. When we incorporate these powerful components in our Christian life, more so than the negative barriers, it's indicative that we're moving with God and all His ways.[1]

We all pray for God to move in our own life, our family's life, our friends & neighbors, our jobs, our community, our country, our church, and abroad. We want to see the power of God at work and change taking place for His good. God moves in our lives for many reasons; to connect with, correct, communicate, convict, counsel, and comfort us through His Spirit. But if we stand still and become complacent, we miss out on spiritual growth and healing opportunities.

However, it's up to us (individually) if we want to move with the presence of His Almighty power, where we can be more aware of His peace, guidance, love, and grace. If you feel distant from God, examine yourself and make sure that the presence of Christ is in your midst.

Paul reminds us in 2 Cor 13:5, "Examine yourselves to see if your faith is genuine. Test yourselves. Surely you know that Jesus Christ is among you; if

1. "What Are Practical Ways to Depend on God Alone."

not, you have failed the test of genuine faith. When we're in Christ—and Him in us, we live, move, and exist in all His ways (Acts 17:27–28).

The extended stay at the foot of Mount Sinai was not a time of idleness; it was a time of great activity in celebration of the goodness and mercy of the Lord. It was also to prepare them for what was expected, and that was the soon triumphal march into the Promise Land. It would be a part of their history, but the key is that they would have to move when God moved.

In his prescribed and appointed time, He moves when He knows it's best, and at all times, we need to be ready. And it's in His perfect timing when we lean upon our Lord and go in motion with Him that we can experience His goodness, lovingkindness, and mercy.

When we are actively in motion with God, we exhibit significant elements in our lives that prove we're leaning more on Him versus our own understanding (Proverbs chapter 3). Below are some examples that will confirm if we're moving with God and He's in our presence.

1) We yield to His Spirit's guidance in all His wisdom and knowledge (Rom 8:26–27).

2) We illustrate patience and faithfulness because we know He's in control (Rom 12:12).

3) We love and long to obey His word (John 14:15).

4) We possess the attitude of Christ (Phil chapter 2).

4) We press on in life with endurance and perseverance (Phil 3:14).

5) We're pursuing life with a Christlike purpose (1 Cor 9:24–26).

6) We make progress through the process (1 Tim 4:15).

7) We rely upon His strength because we know all things are possible through Him (Phil 4:13).

Always remember that moving with God matters—because it keeps us within His proximity, and that should be the prevailing life we live every day. God gave us all functioning parts to help us move forward with Him. Why is this important? If we proceed with our Lord, we will experience more of His peace and joy; it enables us to serve Him and others more. It enlivens our sanctification stages and moves our spiritual needle. It empowers us to persist and persevere and, most importantly, glorifies our God! It matters to Him!

> Gal 5:25, "Since we are living by the Spirit, let us follow the Spirit's leading in every part of our lives."

CHAPTER 10

Godly Communicator

Num 10:1–3, "Now the LORD said to Moses, "Make two trumpets of hammered silver for calling the community to assemble and for signaling the breaking of camp. When both trumpets are blown, everyone must gather before you at the entrance of the Tabernacle."

These instruments were about two feet long with very narrow tubes, and when blown in a certain way, they sent forth a sharp and piercing sound that would communicate clearly to God's children the desired intent. The silver trumpet releases a ringing and joyous sound. And in almost every instance in which the blowing of these trumpets is mentioned in God's word, it suggests gladness, hope, and triumph. They were also blown to announce royal and other ceremonies and occasions of tremendous rejoicing.

The material used and details of these trumpets made of hammered silver probably took longer to complete. Still, their use was of significance. They were used to coordinate the tribes as they moved through the wilderness—orchestrating to keep them in such a formation that there was "clear communication and control." Keeping many people united, uniformed, and organized required a clear and concise message.

Today, the two most important types of communication are between man and God and between human beings. It is more than just our ability to talk, but also to listen. Listening is the first part of that connection as we commune with God. God's primary ways of interfacing with us are through His Word (Rom 10:17) and the Holy Spirit (John 14:26). Our primary mode of communication with God is in prayer, and as believers, we must examine how we converse with our fellow man.

When engaged in a conversation, as we prepare to speak to others, we should ask ourselves these questions:

- Is it the truth? (Zech 8:16)
- Is it filled with lovingkindness (Tit 3:2)?
- Is it necessary (Prov 11:22)?
- Will it be with words of grace (Col 4:6)?
- Is it going to be biblically productive (Col 3:23)?
- Will it glorify God (1 Cor 10:31)?
- And is it building up the body of Christ (Eph 4:1–16)?

Conveying godly communication is when the Spirit of Truth leads us to speak gracefully and encourage others within the body in love and peace.[1] The steps above demonstrate that our motives are in check by the Holy Spirit. As Christians, below are valid points on why clear and accurate communication is essential, biblically.

- First, it can avoid confusion and prevent us from misleading someone scripturally.
- Second, it provides a defined purpose, plan, and objective, keeping everyone on a productive spiritual course.
- Third, it portrays a Christian as someone genuine and believable.
- Fourth, it establishes trust and accountability.
- Fifth, it enables growth and maturity in you and others.
- Sixth, it demonstrates "Who" is leading you in how you orchestrate your communication.
- And seventh, it glorifies God when we iterate a biblical message to others on His behalf—as His ambassadors. It could be that one conversation that leads someone to Christ!

Poor, immoral, and inaccurate communication can break down, demotivate, and discourage anyone. That is why it is essential to hear from God first to know that our hearts, souls, and minds align with Him. We must ensure that the Spirit is alive and active in us. Remember, our Christlike approach is crucial, so we should possess godly wisdom, knowledge, and discernment beforehand in communicating with others.

---

1. "What the Bible Says About Communication."

When our words, deeds, and approach align with Christ, it is evident that the Holy Spirit is working within us—because He's the key to our state of gracious and loving Christlike outreach. We can never iterate as representatives of our Lord and Savior unless we've had a heart and mind that's been changed and possesses the same attitude as Jesus Christ. When we are ready to humbly submit and surrender ourselves to Him, the power of the Holy Spirit can transform us into godly communicators.

Just think, before we had the power of the Holy Spirit indwelling in our lives, our words were not of love, mercy, and grace but of the flesh that spewed out words of profanity, hate, division, jealousy, greed, and pure selfishness. But as genuine believers in Christ and His word, when we enable His Spirit to work in us, what comes forth are words and acts of love, joy, peace, patience, goodness, kindness, faithfulness, gentleness, and self-control (Gal 5:22–23). This is when the beauty of God's Spirit springs forth a Christlike communicator, motivator, and promoter of nothing but the Truth.

The only way our communication can be Christlike is that it must resemble the words and actions of Christ Himself. Examples: 1) Christ communicated with His Father often through prayer. He was consistently and continually connected with the Father. 2) Jesus spoke the truth. 3) He conveyed His messages out of love and genuine compassion. He had a concern for the spiritual well-being of others. 4) Jesus Christ spoke with humility and grace. If pride and self are part of our communication, it will never hit the point and connect with others! 5) And when Jesus spoke, miraculous things happened that aligned with God's will!

Below are biblical and fruitful steps we can incorporate into our daily lives as godly communicators that align with the same model as Jesus Christ.

- Convey words of praise instead of taking the Lord's name in vain, Ps 150.
- Speak words of truth in love, Eph 4:15.
- Use words of grace, Col 4:6
- Communicate words that build up others; don't spread gossip, Eph 4:29
- Don't complain, Phil 2:14
- Have conversations guided by godly wisdom and discernment, Jas 3:13
- Be quick to listen, slow to speak, and slow to become angry, Jas 1:19

We can only accomplish this in His power, not in our own strength. You can always tell when you're around a godly communicator. Just like their portrayal of humility and gentleness outwardly, the loving words that come from their mouth stem from a genuine heart, soul, and mind. It portrays a faithful

Christian who conveys words of such heavenly eloquence that it is known firsthand, "Who is at work in their daily walk and talk."

> Ps 19:14, "May the words of my mouth and the meditation of my heart be pleasing to you, O LORD, my rock and my redeemer."

CHAPTER 11

Godless Complainer

> Num 11:1-2, "Soon the people began complaining about their hardship, and the LORD heard everything they said. Then the LORD's anger blazed against them, and he sent a fire to rage among them, and he destroyed some of the people in the outskirts of the camp. Then the people screamed to Moses for help, and when he prayed to the LORD, the fire stopped."

This passage clearly shows us that God does not like a complainer. Complaining hearts can displease God, especially when they show little gratitude for what He's done in the past and little faith in what He could do for us now. The people were complaining amongst themselves, and it was apparent that their hearts were dissatisfied!

In this chapter, we even see where Moses got caught up in the nastiness of complaining because of all his dealings with the Israelite's selfish ways. But here's the significant contrast between someone who relies on God versus those who do not. Moses took his matter to Yahweh—Who can resolve all problems.

And that's why God responded to Moses positively versus the people of Israel. Complaining with others can drain everyone physically, mentally, emotionally, and even spiritually, leading to more internal friction and division, which can distance us from God. It is evident that a constant complainer in life is not in connection with God daily—because they are more in tune with their own comfort than God's desires.

How in the world could the Israelites complain so much? After all, they were experiencing the presence of God, His protection and provision, His goodness and mercy, and mighty miracles. We read the stories of the Israelites and wonder how His people, who were so wonderfully blessed, still complain after all God did for them. Yet, they still murmured against Him because of their selfish and ignorant ways. But here are some vital relative points on why they were constantly moaning and groaning:

They were still in the wilderness—not a place the flesh wanted, and their circumstances were difficult in this desolate land. But regardless of the fleshly discomfort, nothing good came out of their habitual complaining. Does this apply to us today? Because let's face it, God does not like a constant complaining and murmuring spirit.

When He places us in a spot out of our comfort zone, He has done it for a reason and purpose. He wants us to grow and become like His Son, Jesus Christ. Would we grow spiritually if we had everything we wanted on a silver platter? If we get too complacent and satisfied in our earthly life, it will never nourish a healthy soul and spirit that can be useful for His services. We cannot glorify a Holy Lord when it's all about our "whole self."

Later in this chapter, we also see a powerful passage where God asked Moses to bring leaders to Him who were worthy of the call because of their wisdom, conduct, and ministry to others. He would come down and cast some of the Spirit that was upon Moses onto these called servicemen.

In doing this, they will be able to carry the people's burdens and assist Moses. God is coming to the aid of His servant so that these other servicemen will bear the responsibility of the people along with Moses. Now, he will not have to carry it alone—for these godly men would support and strengthen Moses by assisting him with this seemingly heavy spiritual load. It was evident that God's faithful servant was getting weighed down by all the people's complaining ways.

But here's the key: These leaders must have the same heart, the same vision, and the same Spirit that was on Moses. If not, there would be no agreement among the leadership of the nation—and disaster could come to Israel. It was crucial that they were all on the same page and aligned with God! And this is how God works amongst His body of believers today! How does this apply to a complaining spirit? Glad you asked.

A complaining person is of no use to God. Why? Because they don't have the same heart, vision, and spirit as God. They don't instill godly wisdom and conduct and could never minister to people who need help in many ways. Unfortunately, they are more disabling than enabling. And here's a huge gut punch; they are depriving the Holy Spirit of empowering their God-given gifts for the Lord's work because the flesh consumes them way too much!

We don't have to be an elder or deacon to be of service to the Lord. He does not care about the title or position. He wants a genuine, selfless, and empathetic heart for others that want to be of use for the building of His Kingdom.

As believers, we are challenged "to not" possess a complaining spirit (Phil 2:14–15; 1 Pet 4:9). Instead, we are to love one another so that we may become "blameless and pure" in God's eyes. If we constantly grumble and complain, it shows how worldly we still are (Jas 4:1–3).

A complaining spirit is constantly challenging, continuously critical, confrontationally cruel, a creator of chaos & confusion, carelessly crippling & cutting others down—because they are crafty, cunning, and combative. These types of people have "unfulfilled desires." One evangelist says it with such volume—" A continuously complaining spirit has broken their faith in God. If we must complain, let it be to the One about our sinful ways and put within us a new heart, one that rejoices rather than complains."

A chronic complainer can burden so many people within their proximity. They want to shift their burdens on others, which can debilitate us in many ways. A whimpering groaner in everyday life could never bear the responsibility of someone else's load because their bandwagon is overflowing with self. They could care less about the weight of other people's burdens because they possess a selfish one-track mind and heart. They are fixated and obsessively absorbed with themselves. And the power punch is this—at the heart of a complaining spirit is a load of selfishness that leads one to desire their ways over others and even God. It can lead a person to despise submission and humility, which is dangerous.

We must realize, as Christians, that many people in our own little communities carry all types of worries, anxieties, fears, doubts, chaos, confusion, discontentment, uncertainties, hopelessness, failure, guilt, sin, trauma, division, and feeling distant from God. The list of burdens could stretch for miles, but the "weariness of one" can bog anyone down into a pit of despair. With this type of load in any person's life, how could a complaining spirit, who is all about themselves, assist anyone for the glory of God? Paul reminds us in Phil 2:14–16 that a complaining and argumentative person is more harmful than helpful.

If the people who are struggling in these areas listed above, how can we, as a body, represent the church and Christ if we're continuously arguing, complaining, gossiping, and spewing out more negativity than a positive Christlike outlook in life? Trust me, when we fall to the vices of the enemy, we will always lack the unifying power of Christ in our personal lives and even in the church. Therefore, our Holy God challenges us to strive for righteousness so we can be set apart for effective use in our homes, community, and church.

As part of the family of God, we are to come to the aid of our brothers and sisters in need (Phil 2:3–4). If we carry a garbage truck of pride and self-ishness and desire our ways more than others, we miss the invitation to assist someone when their load suddenly becomes too heavy. Remember, we are to bear one another's burdens, but we can't if our "self-truck" is overloaded.

Our challenge in life today is simply this: to commit to Christ willingly and lovingly, which means taking up our cross daily, giving up our hopes, dreams, possessions, and even our very life if needed for the cause of Christ. Only if we willingly take up our cross can we be called His true disciples (Luke 14:27). The reward is worth the price, not temporal, but eternal. Remember, as Jesus called His disciples to "take up your cross and follow Me," He, too, bore a cross. Our Lord led the way, and that's a great challenge in our daily lives. Give up self for His sake; it's worth the cause!

> Matt 16:23–25, "Jesus turned to Peter and said, "Get away from me, Satan! You are a dangerous trap to me. You are seeing things merely from a human point of view, not from God's." Then Jesus said to his disciples, "If any of you wants to be my follower, you must give up your own way, take up your cross, and follow me. If you try to hang on to your life, you will lose it. But if you give up your life for my sake, you will save it."

I would much rather surround my life with an "optimist happy camper" than a 'pessimistic, nitpicking nagger.'

CHAPTER 12

God's Humble

Num 12:1–8, "While they were at Hazeroth, Miriam, and Aaron criticized Moses because he had married a Cushite woman. They said, "Has the LORD spoken only through Moses? Hasn't He spoken through us, too?" But the LORD heard them. (Now Moses was very humble—humbler than any other person on earth.) So immediately, the LORD called to Moses, Aaron, and Miriam and said, "Go out to the Tabernacle, all three of you!" So, the three of them went to the Tabernacle. Then the LORD descended in the pillar of cloud and stood at the entrance of the Tabernacle. "Aaron and Miriam!" He called, and they stepped forward. And the LORD said to them, "Now listen to what I say: "If there were prophets among you, I, the LORD, would reveal myself in visions. I would speak to them in dreams. But not with my servant Moses. Of all my house, he is the one I trust. I speak to him face to face, clearly, and not in riddles! He sees the LORD as He is. So why were you not afraid to criticize my servant, Moses?"

Interestingly, Aaron and Miriam criticized Moses and his wife over something that she had no control over, which was her appearance. Either because she was an Ethiopian (a black or dark African) or had a dark complexion. As we see in the following verses, the complaint over Moses' wife was not the real issue.

Like then, and even today, many people are criticized over a matter that is not the real issue—because many of us often argue over minor disagreements. But here's a key takeaway, when people argue over the most minute matter, there's apparently a more significant issue within them.[1]

1. "Numbers 12—The Dissension of Aaron and Miriam."

This passage is so powerful in its message because it shows us how the Lord will stand up for His humble servants. Apparently, Miriam and Aaron were filled with envy and pride because of Moses' leadership role. They could not find fault with Moses as a leader, so they chose to criticize his wife. They diverted from the real issue, which stemmed from the root of their pride. This apparent smoke screen did not hold up with Almighty God—because we can't fool Him, He read right through them. He "immediately" called them to meet Him in the Tabernacle when he overheard them. Look at God's profound words to Moses' brother and sister:

"Of all my house, he (Moses) is the one I trust. I speak to him face to face, clearly, and not in riddles! He sees the LORD as He is." God had his humble and faithful servants' back! Just like God can see through a person with the wrong motives, He also knows His humble and loyal servants' hearts. This proves that our Loving and Just God will always come to the aid of His committed ones—because He knows that their motives and desires align with His will and plan.

Nothing pleases and delights the Lord more than a humble heart because it's rooted in faith, love, and obedience. As much as He opposes pride, always remember that God rewards humility. In Psalm 25:9, we see that humility is rewarded with God's guidance and wisdom—and this is important for us today because we need this to know His will and purpose in life.

God values and desires a humble person because it denotes a broken spirit and a contrite heart. This type of heart set and spirit nourishes a sorrowful person, leading them to seek the Lord persistently. They possess a joy that is second to none because they know where their forgiveness comes from, which leads to restoration and favor with God. They don't expect anything in return, but it's the power of the Holy Spirit constantly working out their salvation with fear and trembling (Phil 2:12–13).

So, what is our reaction or response when someone attacks us, as in the passage above? Do we succumb to the flesh and act out of anger or seek vengeance? Or do we lean upon the Holy Spirit's guidance and heed His advice? It is humanly impossible to act out of humility when the flesh generates the onslaught of our words and actions. We can only perform Christlike humility with the help of the Holy Spirit—leaning upon His word and guidance. Then we will see ourselves responding more with patience and graciousness versus reactions of hatefulness.

One way of instilling humility in our lives is knowing who we are in Christ because He's the model of humility (Philippians chapter 2). Remember, apart from Him, we cannot accomplish anything (John 15:5). When we know that His ways are our ways, His truth is our bedrock, and His life is our ultimate lifeline, that is evidence that we're His branch grafted into the True Vine.

Jesus teaches us in the gospel of John chapter 15 that He cuts off every branch that doesn't produce fruit, and He prunes the branches that bear so that they can produce even more. You see, the branch that's part of the True Vine has submitted themselves entirely to His workshop for fine-tuning because a humble, ready, willing, and loving servant wants to do more for the Lord. They will swallow their pride and self to get to the level of fruitfulness for His glory.

Clear trademarks of a humble Christlike servant portray and convey themselves in these manners below:

1. They speak less about themselves and more of others (Phil 2:3, 1 Cor 10:24).

2. They are encouragers, not discouragers (Eph 4:29, 1 Thess 5:11).

3. They want to manage the affairs of God's work biblically (1 Tim 3:5).

4. They're not nosy and don't get wrapped up in the busyness of everyone else because they are in the "business of God" (1 Thess 4:11).

5. They don't point their fingers and look at the mistakes of others. Instead, they look in the mirror at their own weaknesses and opportunities, holding themselves accountable. When they do this, they will point out the strengths of others (Jas 1:17–27, Rom 14:12).

6. They accept constructive criticism like a soldier of Christ should (2 Timothy chapter 2).

7. When attacked or provoked, they embody the Fruit of the Spirit with acts of love, joy, peace, patience, kindness, goodness, faithfulness, gentleness, and self-control (Gal 5:22–23).

Is this easy? Absolutely not! That's why Jesus tells us to abide in Him, and He will abide in us, for apart from Him, we can do nothing. Humility is a core Christian value that should be lived out in every believer's life. It is the master key to how Christians relate to each other—for it's the bond to unity. It's the foundation for a healthy church and reflects our most profound understanding of what God has done for us. When we grasp this, our self takes a backseat, and Christ is back in the front, steering our course in life.

> Eph 4:2–3, "Always be humble and gentle. Be patient with each other, making allowance for each other's faults because of your love. Make every effort to keep yourselves united in the Spirit, binding yourselves together with peace."

CHAPTER 13

Godly Messenger

Num 13:17–20, 25–28, "Moses gave the men these instructions as he sent them out to explore the land: "Go north through the Negev into the hill country. See what the land is like and find out whether the people living there are strong or weak, few or many. See what kind of land they live in. Is it good or bad? Do their towns have walls, or are they unprotected like open camps? Is the soil fertile or poor? Are there many trees? Do your best to bring back samples of the crops you see." (It happened to be the season for harvesting the first ripe grapes.)" After exploring the land for forty days, the men returned to Moses, Aaron, and the whole community of Israel at Kadesh in the wilderness of Paran. They reported to the whole community what they had seen and showed them the fruit they had taken from the land. This was their report to Moses: "We entered the land you sent us to explore, and it is indeed a bountiful country—a land flowing with milk and honey. Here is the kind of fruit it produces. But the people living there are powerful, and their towns are large and fortified. We even saw giants there, the descendants of Anak!"

God had commanded Moses to send the twelve spies so the Israelites would be equipped to do battle in the land. Even though God would ultimately fight the battles for them, they had to do their part, which was to move forward in faith. Moses told the people of the goodness of the land (Exod 13:5), but he still needed more information about the people, the cities, and the landscape before the people could enter the Promise Land. So, he took careful steps to get the required information he needed. No doubt, Moses' prudent measures were led by the wisdom of God.

God's chosen ones are going to receive a blessing beyond their comprehension. Still, their steps into this blessing have requirements" Move forward in faith" and let the Lord take care of your battles. In other words, "Trust Me!" God delights in the one who follows Him, trusts Him, and sets out to do His will—because in all His protection and provisions, God watches over them and makes firm every step that person takes.

Even though they will stumble—they will not fall because God holds them by the hand (Ps 37:23–24). It's when we yield to God's advice and align our steps and plans with His is when the wisdom of God takes root within each one of us and produces a fruit of good deeds, James 3:17.

God had already told His children that this new land was rich and fertile, flowing with milk and honey. He even said this land was bountiful and would be their own possession. Wasn't God's word and His promise enough? Apparently not! With all the richness this Land had to offer, most spies focused on one thing—their adversaries—the giants in the land.

With all the positive attributes this land provided, they only focused on the "one negative," the giants they would have to confront. In their mind, because the giants were so large, they perceived them as powerful. After all the miracles and incredible power, they witnessed firsthand by Almighty God, "one negative view (in their fleshly eyes)" consumed their entire thought process.

Remember this story? For 40 days, morning and evening, the Philistine Giant Goliath strutted in front of the Israelite army, taunting them, intimidating them, harassing them, laughing at them, and daring them to come to defeat him. Until one man who was fearless, faithful, and after God's own heart—who did not have a physical chance to stand up and defeat this giant came forth. And David had a powerful message from God for the enemy that many Christians know by heart. "I come to you in the name of Almighty God whom you have defied, and today the Lord will conquer you! It is His battle, 'David said,' and the Lord will give you to us."

Therefore, we must ingrain into our heart, soul, and mind that our confidence is in God, who will fight our battles and bring us safely home (Jude 1:24–25). No matter the persecution we may go through and even that one negative perception—we cannot allow it to consume us to the point of feeling helpless and hopeless. God is always on our side and with us (Rom 8:31–34)! If God is for us, who can be against us?

But isn't it amazing how only "two" of the twelve spies sent out to scope the land God promised would come back with positive and exciting news? But most of these twelve spies saw something completely different. Their weak eyes would behold such a fear that their negative news would spread like a virus throughout the nation; they would send a message that was not of God. Even after God told them, He would be with them every step of the way, fighting their battles, and the land they were going to inherit was full of so many riches; it did not seem to be enough.

We see some key points at work in this storyline: 1) God kept His promise and was giving them a land of such richness, 2) He would be with them, 3) He would fight their battles, 4) God used two godly men to come back with a positive outlook on life, 5) One of the godly messengers even said with boldness and confidence, "let's go and take the land," 6) But ten came back with such fear of their enemies they spread the bad report to others, 7) And their negative insight set such a fear in the people of the nation they cried out and eventually rebelled.

If we see the first five points, we see a vast amount of positive information that anyone in their right spiritual mind would move forward in faith. Still, the latter two would be the predominant force, eventually leading to more problems. The weight of the two negatives outweighed the five key positives. We cannot allow the minor difficulties in life to blind us to the power of God's help, promises, and provisions. The enemy always does his best to obscure our vision from the Goodness of God!

This is a classic example and perfect illustration of the importance for believers as God's messengers. In a society of people who are blinded and focus too much on all the negativities, false information, and conspiracy theories, we need to hear more of the message of the Good News. After all, God's messengers honor, exalt, and proclaim God's laws, not that of man. They teach the will of the One who sent them (John 7:16) and are the ones He entrusted to preach His words (John 6:29; 3:34).

Some of the most critical events in the history of redemption involve God sending messages to His servants through the angels. Consider, for example, the birth of Jesus, when the angel Gabriel announced the birth of John the Baptist to Zechariah and the birth of the Savior to Mary (Luke 1:5–38).

The interchange between Gabriel and Zechariah is remarkable. Gabriel struck Zechariah with great fear, which tells us how rare it was for angels to appear to human beings (verses 5–12). We also see Gabriel exercising authority over Zechariah, telling him he must name his son "John" and that John must not consume strong drinks (verses 13–17). This authority does not belong to Gabriel inherently, but the angel possesses it because he has a message sent from God.

When angels speak on behalf of the Lord, their message carries the weight of His authority. The same is true of the prophets and Apostles who wrote sacred Scripture. We hold the Bible as our only infallible authority and ultimate arbiter of truth because God inspires it, and its writings speak on behalf of the Lord (2 Tim. 3:16–17).

And look at the dialogue between Mary and Gabriel because it is striking. She hears she is to be the mother of the Messiah, the One who will sit on David's throne and give victory to His people (Luke 1:26–38). As such, Jesus is the greatest messenger from God. He brings a message—the Gospel—but He is far greater than any other messenger. He is, in fact, God Himself, and He took on human flesh in order to speak the Word of God to His people (John 1:1–18).

When we represent our Lord, as His messengers, to a society and culture fed more on untruths, we must be clear, accurate, and genuine messengers on His behalf. And remember what Jesus told us in John 14:12, "I tell you the truth, anyone who believes in me will do the same works I have done, and even greater works because I am going to be with the Father."

Jesus was not saying that every believer would walk on water, raise the dead and do the exact works of His Apostles, but God's work will continue in the world through you and me. Even after Jesus' earthly ministry ended, His work would go on. Followers of Jesus Christ, empowered by the Holy Spirit, would continue to help people and spread the Gospel. No matter what your gift is, God will use it in a fashion and powerful way that will resonate and permeate throughout your community for God's glory.

Here are some key characteristics of being a godly messenger:

- Is a new person in Christ and a devout ambassador, 2 Cor 5:17–20

- Is a peacemaker, Rom 14:19

- Is an encourager and builds up others, 1 Thess 5:11

- Is a representative honoring Jesus Christ, Col 3:17

- Is a loving and obedient student of God's word, teaching the truth, 2 Tim 3:16–17

- Possesses the attitude of Christ, Phil chapter 2

- Is a living sacrifice unto His service, Rom 12:1–2

- Utilizing their gifts for the Lord and His glory, 1 Peter 4:10–11

- Embodies the Fruit of the Spirit, Gal 5:22–23

- They are Kingdom Builders, Eph 2:10, Rom 14:17

These are ten vital elements that characterize a devoted godly messenger. They joyously embrace this because they are not ashamed to proclaim the name of Jesus Christ—no matter who they are around—and where they are.

At some point and time, there could be growing pains in their profound proc-lamation around family and friends and even others, but the efforts are worth it because that is what God has called us to do. Although it is not believed that Thomas Paine was a Christian, he is known for some striking quotes that parallel the godly messenger that is so needed today.

- "He who dares not offend cannot be honest."

- "Those who expect to reap the blessings of freedom must, like men, un-dergo the fatigues of supporting it."

- "The harder the conflict, the more glorious the triumph. What we obtain too cheap, we esteem too lightly; dearness only gives everything its value. I love the man that can smile in trouble, that can gather strength from distress and grow."

In all we do as godly messengers for our Lord today, we must stay true to His word and teachings and never waver from its basic principles. When we're in that close-knit relationship with Christ through His word and Spirit, we grow and learn how to present our message of the Gospel. We cannot afford to cave into this culture's public opinion and pressures and allow it to distort our biblical thought processes. If we do—we're misrepresenting our Savior.

Paul stood faithful to God regardless of whether the people praised or slandered him. He was constant in his joy and contentment in being the godly messenger God intended him to be. Despite his hardships, circumstances, and challenging stages, he stood firm and accurate to the Good News of Christ. He refused to compromise the Godly standards of sharing the message of Christ, and for that, he will be rewarded. What an esteemed honor, even for you and me.

2 Cor 6:4–10, "In everything we do, we show that we are true ministers of God. We patiently endure troubles and hardships and calamities of every kind. We have been beaten, been put in prison, faced angry mobs, worked to exhaustion, endured sleepless nights, and gone without food. We prove ourselves by our purity, our understanding, our patience, our kindness, by the Holy Spirit within us, and by our sincere love. We faithfully preach the truth. God's power is working in us. We use the weapons of righteousness in the right hand for attack and the left hand for defense. We serve God whether people honor us or despise us, whether they slander us or praise us. We are honest, but they call us impostors. We are ignored, even though we are well known. We live close to death, but we are still alive. We have been beaten, but we have not been killed. Our hearts ache, but we always have joy. We are poor, but we give spiritual riches to others. We own nothing, and yet we have everything."

CHAPTER 14

Disgruntled Lives

Num 14:17–23, "Please, Lord, prove that your power is as great as you have claimed. For you said, 'The Lord is slow to anger and filled with unfailing love, forgiving every kind of sin and rebellion. But he does not excuse the guilty. He lays the sins of the parents upon their children; the entire family is affected—even children in the third and fourth generations.' In keeping with your magnificent, unfailing love, please pardon the sins of this people, just as you have forgiven them ever since they left Egypt." Then the Lord said, "I will pardon them as you have requested. But as surely as I live, and as surely as the Earth is filled with the Lord's glory, not one of these people will ever enter that land. They have all seen my glorious presence and the miraculous signs I performed both in Egypt and in the wilderness, but again and again, they have tested me by refusing to listen to my voice. They will never even see the land I swore to give their ancestors. None of those who have treated me with contempt will ever see it."

Moses pleaded with God, asking Him to please forgive them. When we see God telling Moses in verse twenty that He will pardon them, we see the divine characteristics of God come to the surface, and this is due to the relationship that the mediator Moses had with God. Because of this unbelievable relationship, we see; 1) The patience of God, 2) His endless love and care for His people, 3) His boundless mercy, 4) He listens to His people when they come to Him in faith and obedience, and 5) God is always faithful to His word.

But also, in this passage, we need to understand that this was not a teaching of generational curses when He said, "He lays the sins of the parents upon their children; the entire family is affected—even children in the third and fourth generations." God repeated the exact words when God gave Moses the ten commandments in Exodus chapter twenty and a new copy of the covenant in Exodus chapter thirty-four.

God is saying He will not tolerate any sin now and in the future; He is consistent, faithful, and true to His word. In Leviticus, God told the people that if they genuinely repent and try to correct their wrongs, He will turn His heart toward them again. In Lev 26:40–42, he says, "But at last my people will confess their sins and the sins of their ancestors for betraying me and being hostile toward me. When I have turned their hostility back on them and brought them to the land of their enemies, *then at last, their stubborn hearts will be humbled,* and they will pay for their sins. Then I will remember my covenant with Jacob and my covenant with Isaac and my covenant with Abraham, and I will remember the land."

Also, a keynote, in some Jewish homes and even in the wilderness, it's said by many scholars that there could have been three or four generations of Israelites, which explains the detail of this passage. But the central point was this—God constantly saw their behavior pattern and made it crystal clear that He would not let future generations' sins go unnoticed.

God's word also reminds us in Gal 3:13, "Christ rescued us from the curse pronounced by the law. He took it upon Himself the curse for our wrongdoing." This is important for us today because there seems to be a trend in some churches where they cast an attempt to blame every sin and problem on some generational curse. This is not biblical. God's warning to visit iniquity in future generations is part of the Old Testament Law.

We must remember that a generational curse was a consequence for a specific nation (Israel) for a specific sin (idolatry). But to clarify this further is the compassionate and grace-filled gift God offers us through His Son, Jesus. Once a believer accepts Christ as their savior, it breaks the generational curse because we are under a new covenant. Jesus tells us in John 8:34–36, "Very truly I tell you, everyone who sins is a slave to sin. A slave has no permanent place in the family, but a son belongs to it forever. So, if the Son sets you free, you will be free indeed."

Even the prophet Jeremiah shared this Good News of Christ over five hundred years before His birth. He reminds us in Jer 31:29–31, predicting the days to come through God's vision: "The people will no longer quote this proverb: 'The parents have eaten sour grapes, but their children's mouths pucker at the taste.' All people will die for their own sins—those who eat the sour grapes will be the ones whose mouths will pucker. "The day is coming," says the LORD, "when I will make a new covenant with the people of Israel and Judah."

In this powerful passage, the people try and blame God's judgment on the sins of their fathers. Yes, one person's iniquity can affect other people, but everyone is still responsible for the sins in their own life. In God's eyes, there are no excuses and scapegoats for not holding ourselves accountable for acts against Him. After all, He's given us every resource for living a godly life, as Peter reminds us in his second epistle. If we blame anything on anyone because we may be disgruntled about a particular event in our life, we may want to start by looking at ourselves first.

This profound chapter shows us how God will respond to His children who continuously rebel against Him, for they will experience His punishment. Earlier in chapter 14, we saw how the Israelites were so stricken and debilitated by absolute fear that they now would not listen to Moses, Aaron, Joshua, or Caleb. Their minds were made up—they were succumbing to the fear of man and not trusting God. And even this close to the Promise Land, many would never see the land because of their lack of trust and obedience in the Lord. God said, "Because you have complained to Me, none of you who are twenty years or older will enter the land that I swore to give you—now will die in this wilderness!"

The Israelites had as much of a clear view of God's work as anyone. However, His words, blessings, promises, provisions, protection, and presence were insufficient. As a result, they continued to disobey and defy God after all the miraculous things they witnessed. Really! His children continuously failed to trust and obey because of their disgruntled lives—for they lacked trust time after time, leading to disobedience.

They were constant complainers, never content, exhibited acts of anger, were irritable and resentful, repeatedly rebelled against God, and even fell prey to idolatry. It's as if they were sending a message to God, "We're abandoning Your ways and will seek our own desires,"—for their emotions in the flesh got the best of them way too often. He could have quickly left them in the wilderness, but that's not our loving God, for His promise would stand true, and He would be faithful to His word. God does not fail us; we fail Him.

When we fail to trust God, it can often bring us even greater problems than we initially faced. When we run from God's truth and His word, we will run into more problems. Our lack of faith is almost like calling God a liar because He tells us in His word that He is with us and He's faithful and true. That is why God instructed the new generation of Israelites before going into the Promise Land to continually remind themselves of what God had done for them:

"And these words that I command you today shall be in your heart. You shall teach them diligently to your children and shall talk of them when you sit in your house, and when you walk by the way, and when you lie down, and when you rise" (Deut 6:6–7). God knows that the spirit is willing, but the flesh is weak (Mark 14:38), so He commands His people to constantly remember these things—which still applies to us today.

Classic emotions and irresponsibility are rampant when our flesh kicks into high gear. Examples: 1) That's just the way I'm wired, 2) That's who I am, 3) That's the way my parents did it, and I will not change for anyone. Really! So often, our deep heritages can be good or bad, but if what we follow in everyday life does not align with God's word and His plans, we are off course.

That physical bloodline from our family DNA can be overpowering and affect our lives in ways that could be detrimental, but there's a spiritual DNA bloodline that trumps all things—and that is who we are in Jesus Christ. If we look at the pattern of the Israelites, we see a nation of people who were never satisfied. Their rebellious ways sent frequent messages of being irate, for they were seemingly unhappy—even with all of God's goodness. What can we learn from them? How can we discover a more content life in God and do more things pleasing to Him?

When a person is disgruntled, dissatisfied, discontented, displeased, and disappointed, they often exhibit anger and rebellion. We see this type of reaction often in the Israelites throughout the Old Testament. God's word tells us they were rebellious, which means they were turbulent, uncontrollable, ungovernable, and unruly. What was the cause? When we peel back all the layers, we see that the Israelites, throughout their history in the Promised Land, struggled with conflict among the tribes.

This disunity went back to the patriarch Jacob, who presided over a house that was divided. The sons of Leah and the sons of Rachel had their share of contention even in Jacob's lifetime (Gen 37:1–11). And when we wind the clock forward to the split of the Kingdom, the division was a judgment on not keeping God's commands, specifically those who were not prohibiting idolatry. The principle is that sin brings division (1 Cor 1:13, 11:18; James 4:1).

When we continuously read about God's chosen ones' hostility amongst themselves, their jealousy, and ongoing conflicts, they were engulfed in their way of life and not God's. They were sending more of a message that they were leaning more toward self than on the power of God. That will always lead to problems. It seems that many of us today have inherited that hideous DNA from the Israelites.

However, we can counter these ugly vices by wanting less of self and more of Christ. Being content and pleased with our lot in life is not based on the externals and all our circumstances—but it has everything to do with God working in us through the power of His Spirit. The Israelite's disgruntled lives are shown through constant complaining, rebelling, and defying God. But we can overcome this by always being grateful, possessing a willing and obedient heart, soul, and mind, and trusting Him.

Disgruntled lives can be disgraceful and a taste of disgust in the eyes of God. Why? Because their deceitful and disturbed spirits lead them to overwhelming discouragement and disappointment, which is the opposite of God's goodness. When heavily focused on life's disappointments, we are too caught up in the flesh, not the Spirit. These vices are all works of the enemy that can cause people to quit something God has told them to do. It can lead to an ill-spirit, bad decisions, and even sin. After all, isn't God good all the time? Always remember what Proverbs 3:1–6 says,

"My child, never forget the things I have taught you. Store my commands in your heart. If you do this, you will live many years, and your life will be satisfying. Never let loyalty and kindness leave you! Tie them around your neck as a reminder. Write them deep within your heart. Then you will find favor with both God and people, and you will earn a good reputation. Trust in the LORD with all your heart; do not depend on your own understanding. Seek his will in all you do, and he will show you which path to take."

The best counter to a disgruntled life is when we remember this—when the Prince of Peace—King of kings, Jesus Christ, will reign forever, and all anger, rebellion, hostility, jealousy, and conflict will be put to rest once and for all. Satan was broken when Christ died on the cross, he has no authority, but he can still deceive and trick us. But he cannot make us do anything. Our Lord has allowed us to choose between life and death, blessings or curses.

Deuteronomy 24:16 and Ezekiel 18:2 reminds us that we cannot blame our parents, past generations, or even the enemy for our sin. Each of us is held individually accountable for our choices in life, so make it count, which will show your true bloodline. This is so important for genuine believers today because there is a day coming when there will be no more unhappiness and displeasure in life—but a time of complete joy and delight!

> 1 Thess 5:15–20, "See that no one pays back evil for evil, but always try to do good to each other and to all people. Always be joyful. Never stop praying. Be thankful in all circumstances, for this is God's will for you who belong to Christ Jesus. Do not stifle the Holy Spirit. Do not scoff at prophecies, but test everything that is said. Hold on to what is good. Stay away from every kind of evil."

CHAPTER 15

Godly Reminders

Num 15:37–41, "Then the LORD said to Moses, "Give the following instructions to the people of Israel: Throughout the generations to come you must make tassels for the hems of your clothing and attach them with a blue cord. When you see the tassels, you will remember and obey the Lord's commands instead of following your own desires and defiling yourselves, as you are prone to do. The tassels will help you remember that you must obey all my commands and be holy to your God. I am the LORD your God who brought you out of the land of Egypt that I might be your God. I am the LORD your God!"

The tassels were a reminder to the people to remember all of God's commands. He wanted them to flee from the desires that separated them from His will and not be self-centered—but to do the opposite of the ways of the world as His children. And no matter what, be faithful and true to the One Living God.

The pagan gods' misguided people and led them down a path that life could be fulfilling if they chased after happy fortunes, prosperity, possessions, power, prestige, and other personal successes. These were all self-centered focuses on a life opposite God's intent.

Because what He desires is a life of selflessness and faithful service to Him and then to others. God wanted His children to serve Him for Who He was, what He had done, and what He was going to do. And if they had the right heart, they would not expect anything in return but honor God and remember what He's doing in the lives of His children.

That cord of blue symbolized the most profound truth in the life of that nation because they were under the direct governance of God's heavenly realm. Every time their eyes would rest on that simple sign, their hearts should be reminded of the supreme truth of their ownership, which is God. Blue was chosen for a purpose. It associated this color with other areas of holiness. The ark of the covenant was covered with a blue cloth, blue curtains adorned the tabernacle, and blue was in the high priest's garments—it was full of holy reminders. Such things can remind us of who we are and who we belong to and provide a kind of "walking accountability" for our daily conduct.[1]

With that in mind. Have we placed Christlike reminders in our daily life—those little things that prompt our godly purpose and plan for today? A simple reminder of Whom we belong to and why we're here? What is the key to these daily reminders? Simply this, "Be still and know that I am God"! Ps 46:10.

When we are still and completely surrendered to Him alone, we find peace even when the Earth gives way to its crazy course in life, where the nations go into an uproar and kingdoms fall—like we're seeing today! When life gets overwhelming and busyness takes priority, remember Ps 46:1, "God is our refuge and strength, an ever-present help in trouble." We must remind ourselves that anyone can run to Him anytime and anywhere.

Why is it essential for us to set reminders in our daily lives of our Creator? First, we need to remember all He's done for us, what He did for us through Christ, and what He will do for you and me in the future. It's vital because our flesh is so weak. We can easily forget our Lord when we get caught up in the busyness of daily routines, the hustles and bustles of life, and distracted by personal, local, and world events. It's not intentional; it's simply the distractions thrown our way by the enemy.

While we so easily forget Him, our Lord never forgets who we are and what we mean to Him. He wants us to constantly remind ourselves that He is our Heavenly Father, who created us in His image in all His wondrous ways and values us deeply. He knows us all so well, and He realizes that it's easy for us to forget Him, so He helps to remind us through His word and the power of His Spirit.

In 2 Pet 1:12–13, He reminds us, "Therefore, I will always remind you about these things—even though you already know them and are standing firm in the truth you have been taught. And it is only right that I should keep reminding you as long as I live. For our Lord Jesus Christ has shown me that I must soon leave this earthly life, so I will work hard to make sure you always remember these things after I am gone."

The main reason why we consistently forget is because our mindset is not focused and fixed upon the realities of Heaven (Col 3:1–2). We're more

1. "Numbers 15—Various Laws and Provisions."

in tune with the world and our own personal matters. We all know that the enemy wants to obscure our vision and blind us to the Goodness of God. So, we all need a balance of priority in our daily life, and we can achieve this by incorporating time with God first in His word and through prayer, followed by our life schedule—while thinking about God's blessings and thanking Him continuously throughout each day. Talk about the Lord in the morning with family and friends and in the evenings about His greatness because this embeds Him deep in our thoughts. And when we go to bed at night, we need to have a rooted mind and heart in His Supremacy.

God's word reminds us in Ps 1:1–3, "Oh, the joys of those who do not follow the advice of the wicked, or stand around with sinners, or join in with mockers. But they delight in the law of the Lord, meditating on it day and night. They are like trees planted along the riverbank, bearing fruit each season. Their leaves never wither, and they prosper in all they do." We all get the excellent opportunity to exercise our free will each day—where our choices will fall under one of the two categories: the direction of our flesh or His Spirit.

When we choose to engulf our lives in His word, it will bear fruit that reminds us of His active Spirit working in us. We follow and remember our Lord by thinking about His word, all its power, blessings, guidance, provisions, and protection. This means that we don't only read His word and post a devotion on social media telling our little world that we did our Christlike duty for today and go on our merry way. No! It means we observe God's word, interpret it, and determine how it can be applied. When we do this, we're actively enforcing the knowing and thinking about His word and its life application.

Also nestled in the power of this passage is this: The more we delight in obeying God daily, the more fruitful our lives are for His glory. I cannot count the times when the activities of world events would consume my mind, especially if it were a sensitive topic. In that moment, my emotions go haywire and get out of line. I am now more focused on something that may lead me to say or act in a manner that is not pleasing to God. God cares deeply about our thoughts and attitudes because they can be vital for spiritual nourishment. When we apply the wisdom of God's word into our lives, it will spring out a fountain of fruit that is pleasing to Him.

That's why we must have the Word of God in our hearts and minds so that it rules and governs our spirit each moment of every day through the power of His Spirit. Solomon reminds us in Proverbs chapter 3 that we should never forget the things we were taught; we're to store His commands in our hearts and never let the loyalty and kindness of God escape us. We're told that the best way to remember these words is to wear them like a necklace, write them deep within our hearts, and we will find favor with God and gain a good reputation.

When we store up His words in our hearts and lean on His power, we're prone to sin less (Ps 119:11) and not fall or drift away (Ps 37:31). But when we take our minds and hearts off God, that will open the door and allow the enemy to get a foothold on our hearts—and what right-minded believer would want this?

The key to remembering God daily hinges on this biblical fact: "Our genuine fear of God." This type of fear shows that we adore and revere Him in every facet of our life. It brings forth wisdom, knowledge, discernment, and a fruit-bearing life of godliness that will supersede anything this world of man-made fear throws our way. Biblical fear of the Lord is an awareness that you are in the presence of a holy and Almighty God and that He will hold you accountable for your motives, thoughts, words, and actions.

To fear God is the desire to live in harmony with His righteous standards and to honor Him in everything we say and do. This type of fear ingrained in our hearts, souls, and minds will always have God on our daily checklist. One of the incredible by-products of a genuine fear of God is humility. Because when someone truly fears God, they yearn for more of Him—not self and the ways of the world. They will always yield to God's ways—no matter what. This type of person is in absolute awe of Who He is, and they tremble before His presence daily and want to please Him in all their words and deeds.

But one of the most profound ways to keep our minds and hearts in remembrance of God is when we utilize our God-given gifts daily. When we deploy the beauty of our gifts, we steward God's grace in every moment of our active lives. We're consistently glorifying and exalting Him because we're doing the one thing we're commissioned to do: Spreading the Good News and building up His church body in unity!

When our gifts are at work, we know our purpose, which brings a gratifying heart, mind, and soul that reminds us daily—we're here for a reason and calling. When we're actively feeding the flame on those gifts, it helps us live our daily lives according to His will and plan for the cause of Christ. This affects us, the body, and most importantly, our Creator!

> 1 Cor 11:1–2, "And you should imitate me, just as I imitate Christ. I am so glad that you always keep me in your thoughts, and that you are following the teachings I passed on to you."

CHAPTER 16

God Responds

Num 16:1–7, 19–21, "One day Korah son of Izhar, a descendant of Kohath son of Levi, conspired with Dathan and Abiram, the sons of Eliab, and On son of Peleth, from the tribe of Reuben. They incited a rebellion against Moses, along with two hundred and fifty other leaders of the community, all prominent members of the assembly. They united against Moses and Aaron and said, "You have gone too far! The whole community of Israel has been set apart by the LORD, and he is with all of us. What right do you have to act as though you are greater than the rest of the LORD's people?" When Moses heard what they were saying, he fell face down on the ground. Then he said to Korah and his followers, "Tomorrow morning, the LORD will show us who belongs to him and who is holy."

"The LORD will allow only those whom he selects to enter his own presence. Korah, you and all your followers must prepare your incense burners. Light fires in them tomorrow and burn incense before the LORD. Then we will see whom the LORD chooses as his holy one. You Levites are the ones who have gone too far!" …" Meanwhile, Korah had stirred up the entire community against Moses and Aaron, and they all gathered at the Tabernacle entrance. Then the glorious presence of the LORD appeared to the whole community, and the LORD said to Moses and Aaron, "Get away from all these people so that I may instantly destroy them!"

This profound chapter illustrates God's absolute displeasure when people incite rebellion, which can also lead to division amongst His children. Korah and his comrades witnessed the advantages of priesthood in Egypt with the extraordinary wealth, esteem, and political influence they possessed. They longed for those fleshly accolades again, so they started to conspire for the same lead role in the nation.

But one key area that Korah and his henchman failed to understand was this—they were blind to Moses' ultimate ambition and desire to serve God faithfully, first & foremost. While Moses had pure intentions driven by God, Korah and his friends' impure and immoral thoughts and acts would be their demise. Moses' discerning spirit saw right through their inappropriate ambition and greed, for their motives were not even closely related to the ways of God.

Korah was apparently "not content with his current role of service for the Lord," he wanted more, which led him to stir up his own divisive plan. Korah was so enwrapped in his selfish desires that rebellion consumed him, and his vainness would lead to his destruction. Korah got too focused on his past life of self and greed, and when seeking an ungodly past, it will never lead to a godly direction in our current life.

When we allow the enemy to lure us to the paths of deception and the ways of the world, they can easily lead us to fall from our proper focus on God's plan and purpose. So, God would put Korah to the test, and he would soon discover that God did not accept him, and he would be separated from the nation—for good!

When man "chooses his own path" that may be popular in the eyes of public opinion, divisiveness and rebellion can set in and break down God's body of holiness and unity! Korah and his associates' revolt against God was inexcusable. God even told the people not to touch their belongings—for if they did—it would show sympathy for their cause and agree with their selfish principle. God would not allow it—and He will not tolerate it today!

And we know the rest of the story of how the Earth swallowed up Korah, his household, and his followers. All the surrounding people fled when they heard their screams. The people cried out, "The Earth will swallow us, too!" Then fire blazed forth from the Lord and burned up the two hundred fifty men offering incense." But God was not done! His wrath would continue, and the people witnessed the destruction of their own people right before their very eyes.

After the Earth swallowed up Korah, his two associates, and their household, the other 250 men who offered incense were burned up because the Lord did not receive their worship. He did not accept their worship because it was not of holiness but "wholeness of self." God appoints people in positions for His glory, not man.

When these two hundred fifty men associated themselves with the likes of Korah (uh-oh), they distanced themselves from God's appointed purpose and plan. They were deceived by one who was not aligned with Yahweh, which would lead to their death. It was evident by their actions that they were not in a relationship with God but with themselves and man.

Seeking God is not always easy, not because God is difficult to find but because our minds are over-saturated with misconceptions, misunderstandings, and deceits planted by the enemy. And not to mention the compounding effects of today's culture and the sinful nature of our own nasty hearts in everyday life—what a mess we can become. (Jer 17:9; Jas 1:13–15).

But here's the significant part of this story. While Korah's ambitions of greed and selfishness were not aligned with God's way—Korah's sons witnessed the goodness and greatness of God, and their lives were spared. And from them, seven successive generations of serving God took root, writing 11 Psalms', and from this lineage would come Samuel.

When we see and live out God's greatness & goodness in our lives, He will bless us in all His glorious ways! Jeremiah 29:13 says, "You will seek me and find me when you seek me with all your heart." And that's the key—when we "truly" seek God with all our hearts, we're captivated by all His lovingkindness! And this type of heart set leads a person with more of a desire to please God in establishing unity, love, and peace, not disunity. And this is imperative!

Because "division" is the enemy's goal to deceive, divide, and devour us once we stray away from the purpose and plan of God. This vice is his weapon to destroy the church from within when they elude the true foundation of God's biblical teachings. When a church leaves the very structure of God's principles, it's an open-door invitation for the enemy to sneak in and start his destructive work quickly. But when we're under the authority of Jesus Christ, yielding to His Spirit, grounded in His Truth, unity is rooted and cannot be disrupted.

When division pits a person or group against others and creates discord, disagreements, a difference of opinion, and disputes, you can almost affirm in some way, shape, or form that the enemy is behind it! He wants us to destroy ourselves by focusing on our own "self-desires" and hatred or dislike towards others. Watch out for people like this, for they are only out to appease their own appetite; they are not serving the Lord but their own ambitions!

God's word reminds us in Phil 2:3, "Do nothing out of selfish ambition or vain conceit. Rather, in humility, value others above yourselves." And remember this passage in Col 3:14, "Above all, clothe yourselves with love, which binds us all together in perfect harmony."

So often, when we're off course, God will respond to us and get our attention. "He chastises those He loves," so don't take it wrong because He wants us to be aligned with His purpose and plan (Hebrews chapter 12). He's appointed us right where we are for a reason. He's not done with you and me—He's still connecting our dots with all His grace, mercy, and love He abounds in our lives so we can share it with others; for His glory!

The active dots in our life are through our gifts and talents, prayer, helping others, applying His word, and simply being still and knowing He's God. In all His empowering grace, He's reaching out to you and me, encouraging, guiding, and leading us down a path of His righteousness that brings oneness with Him.

If we feel like a plan has been disrupted and we're feeling restless, distant, uneasy, confused, discomfort, defeated, disappointed, and maybe the unexplainable, more than likely, He's trying to get your attention. Don't lose heart, for as His accepted ones; He's instructing us in His righteousness. 2 Cor 4:16–17, John 14:27. We just need to be still in the quietness of our spirit and listen to God's subtle and most powerful voice.

Ps 27:11–14, "Teach me how to live, O LORD. Lead me along the right path, for my enemies are waiting for me. Do not let me fall into their hands. For they accuse me of things I've never done; with every breath, they threaten me with violence. Yet I am confident I will see the LORD's goodness while I am here in the land of the living. Wait patiently for the LORD. Be brave and courageous. Yes, wait patiently for the LORD." He will respond in His timing, which will always be for our good!

CHAPTER 17

A Servant's Instrument

Num 17:5, 10, "Buds will sprout on the staff belonging to the man I choose. Then I will finally end the people's murmuring and complaining against you." And the LORD said to Moses: "Place Aaron's staff permanently before the Ark of the Covenant to serve as a warning to rebels. This should put an end to their complaints against me and prevent any further deaths."

God clarifies that the buds that sprout on the staff will be the man He chooses! And once again, the Lord proved Himself faithful to His word and His selected servants. The budding of Aaron's rod was the divinely appointed proof of the establishment of God's royal priesthood.

When faced with dissatisfaction over Aaron's leadership as the high priest and his family as the priestly family, God miraculously caused Aaron's staff to sprout, bud, blossom, and produce ripe almonds overnight. Wow! He took one servant's instrument and showed us that when the power of God engages, it can do wondrous things! This symbolized God's choice in His priesthood in this mind-blowing miracle but also carried a decidedly stern warning.

God would perform this miraculous sign to stop the complaining and murmuring amongst the people and get His point across again. And after this sign, He would start judging those who murmured. Could this be the game-changer? Did His children still want to test God's threshold? Would they stop complaining even after witnessing this miracle and finally wake up and display more fruitfulness in their lives versus "fruitlessness"?

Not only would this be a miraculous sign, but the blossoming of dead wood also spoke of fruitfulness. This spiritual attribute is present when godly authority and leadership are practiced and at work in one's life! So, would the

Israelites rise to the occasion and be the fruitful people God truly desired? Could it be, finally, that the world would see "real" Godly authority in the lives of His chosen ones?

After so many events of God's miraculous hands at work, when would the Israelites ever realize God's unending care and compassion for His chosen ones? From their deliverance in bondage to God destroying the enemies, His constant protection and provision, fulfilling His promise of a land so full of richness, and being in their presence, how could they continue to complain and be blind and ignorant to the signs God so visibly put before them?

And today, we have centuries of evidence, findings, historical studies, and profound and convincing results that align with God's consistent and inerrant word. All of these facts should be consciously visible to you and me that would influence our genuine commitment to Him as the One True God.

However, in all our foolishness, we still desire to go our own way too often. We see His divine work of salvation, help, provision, healing, and lives transformed; we have as much evidence as the Israelites. But do these signs give us enough reason to be His loyal servants using our godly instruments of fruitfulness for His glory today? Is that a gut punch?

Fruit is used as a metaphor in God's word to illustrate the type of produce in our own life. It displays our "real" walk with the Lord, our behaviors, attitudes & choices because it's either good or bad. "If you remain in Me and I in you, you will bear much fruit; apart from Me, you can do nothing" (John 15:5).

True fruitfulness begins in the heart with the Fruit of the Spirit (Gal 5:22–23), starting with love through self-control. Today, we are either displaying Christlikeness or hypocrisy because our works will be tested by fire. Using a different metaphor than fruit, 1 Cor 3:12–14 says, "If anyone builds on this foundation using gold, silver, costly stones, wood, hay or straw, their work will be shown for what it is because the Day will bring it to light. It will be revealed with fire, testing the quality of each person's work. If what has been built survives, the builder will receive a reward. [1]

The real sign of a fruitful and faithful follower of Christ exhibits a genuinely repentant heart, emptied of self, full of His Righteousness, wholeheartedly satisfied & content with what Jesus Christ did. They will continuously illuminate His love and joy through all circumstances in life. Their blossomed life is recognizable and displayed in all His Goodness! Through His Spirit, we can attain this life by bursting forth new growth each day for His glorious fields when we, as His servants, are implementing our God-given instruments.

---

1. "What is the Key to Bearing Fruit as a Christian."

If God's children would come to grips with the profoundness of why God chose us, it may change their level of performance in the type of fruit they are producing for the Master! He reminds us in John 15:16, Jesus says, "You did not choose me, but I chose you and appointed you so that you might go and bear fruit—*fruit that will last.*"

Once we know Christ more and grow in His love and grace, we will understand why He chose us, and that's this; He desires us to demonstrate His character and reciprocate His love, mercy, and grace to everyone. And here's the key: If fruitfulness is Christlikeness, then the fruit we produce in our lives will be Christlike in character, words, and actions. They will be exhibited when He sends us into the world. He chose you and me for that purpose.

His authentic children will display a fruit-bearing life because they are constantly being fed and nurtured by His word and Spirit, which will release a life of fruitfulness. But when we fall into the traps of the enemy, as the Israelites did so often, we get more consumed by personal affairs and the physical state and lose complete sight of the condition of our spiritual position in Christ.

This happens when we take our heart, soul, and mind off the signs of God—which lie in His word, led by the Spirit and our communication to Him through prayer. And when this occurs, our spiritual lives become weak and deficient, and we become more fixed on everything in our external life except for the one that matters: our inner life. Not connecting with His Spirit can affect our worship, fellowship, prayer life, relationships, and work life, leading us to a barren life of no production.

As Christ's branch, we must stay attached to the Vine to stay alive. As His disciples, we must be firmly connected to Him to remain spiritually productive. A branch draws strength, nourishment, protection, and energy from the vine. If it is broken off, it quickly dies and becomes unfruitful. When we neglect our spiritual life, ignore the Word of God, skimp on prayer, and withhold areas of our lives from the scrutiny of the Holy Spirit, we are like a branch broken off the vine, and our lives become fruitless.

A prisoner incarcerated in a state prison on death row can bear more fruit than a preacher or televangelist who is serving more "out of self" than for the Lord. The key is when one surrenders themselves "wholly and humbly to God" in every area of their life, where they can be used entirely for His glory. As fruit is unique to each tree, our fruit is unique to us in our productive lives that can yield significant results as His servants if we use our godly instruments. God knows what He has entrusted to each one of us and what He expects us to do with it (Luke 12:48). Our responsibility before God is to be "faithful with little" so that He can trust us with much, using our spirit-filled instruments for His purpose for more and more each day.

Matt 25:21, "The master was full of praise. 'Well done, my good and faithful servant. You have been faithful in handling this small amount, so now I will give you many more responsibilities. Let's celebrate together!"

CHAPTER 18

Godly Responsibility

> Num 18:1, "Then the LORD said to Aaron: "You, your sons, and
> your relatives from the tribe of Levi will be held responsible for any
> offenses related to the sanctuary. But you and your sons alone will
> be held responsible for violations connected with the priesthood.""

The Levites—who were called to a higher standard in the eyes of God as His
support group for the ministry of the priests would be accountable to God
for anyone or anything that would not follow the protection and safety of His
sanctuary—the holiest place. Once God gives someone headship, they are
held accountable to a higher calling and expectation, especially regarding the
shelter of His holy place. God never gives authority without accountability;
the two always go together. If someone is in leadership at God's providential
direction and others are expected to submit to him, God also has special accountability for that person.[1]

As we continue this journey through the book of Numbers, we see that
God takes care of His own and would provide and give good things to the cho-
sen servants of His house. The office of His priesthood was a gift of His grace;
He gave them a spirit of care and responsibility with helpers and assistance.
He provided for their earthly needs, and most importantly, God gave them the
gift of Yahweh Himself.

God's word reminds us in Num 18:20, "And the Lord said to Aaron, "You
priests will receive no allotment of land or share of property among the people
of Israel. I am your share and your allotment." Wow! I want to think that God's

---

1. "Numbers 18—Laws Pertaining to Priests and Levites."

share of Himself would be enough to motivate anyone to be an accountable and responsible godly leader and servant.

When I read Numbers chapter eighteen, I am reminded of the famous passage in Amos 3:3, where God's word says, "Can two people walk together without agreeing on the direction?" In this passage, we not only see a beautiful parable as God walking with either His nation or an individual, but He's telling us that unless they meet together at an appointed time and place, will they mutually decide when and where they will go, what path will they take and if they will go in unity. Without such consultation and agreement, how could they walk together and agree upon plans; unless they are united in friendship, of the same mind and affection for each other? If not, they could go their separate ways.

The beautiful design of these words in Amos shows us that there is no fellowship without friendship. And without that harmony, there can be no communion, direction, or course in life. As stated, when two come together, there's not only an accountability partner but a firm commitment of responsibility to each other as one—because you have the same common goal. The nation of Israel could not expect God to walk with them, show Himself friendly to them, and continue His favor of blessings and provisions when they continuously walked opposite Him by defying and rebelling against His ways. Yet, God is so patient, merciful, and good!

And just like the Israelites, our call-out today lies upon our response to God through our obedient hearts and will, which can be described as "walking with God." When we're of one mind with God, walking in unity with Him, in sync with His will, purpose, and plan, we're more adept at going His way and being godly responsible for everything we do for His glory.

When we do this, we will be more at peace and in harmony with Him and know our obligation of service to Him. And that unity assures us we align with the duties, tasks, responsibilities, and requirements as a daily Christian. Not just once a week, but daily!

Our responsibilities are foremost to God and not to ourselves. We know this because the greatest commandment is to first love the Lord with all our heart, soul, and mind (Matt 22:37–39), and the second is equally important, which is to love your neighbor as yourself. When these commands are intact in our lives, we will all see the acts of godly responsibility come to the surface. This can only be done through our complete submission to His Spirit and Word. And when this act of faith is in motion, we become:

1) Solid students of the Word (growing)

2) Proclaimers of the Word (spreading)

3) Prepared at all times to share and defend the Word (ready)

4) Patient in His Word (composed and controlled) and

5) Spiritually grounded in His Truths (a portrait of Him consistently working in us).

If our genuine and faithful work is for the Lord and done in His power with guidance, we will accomplish its objective because every good work the believer does has lasting benefits that the Lord Himself promises and guarantees. Jesus tells us, "Behold, I am coming soon! My reward is with me, and I will give to everyone according to what he has done" (Rev 22:12).

Our ultimate responsibility lies in working for the Lord and being Christlike, whether it is in "caring after orphans or widows" (Jas 1:27), giving to the hungry, the needy, visiting those in prison (see Matt 25:35–36), serving in our workplace (see Col 3:22), or whatever we do in word and deed as His true representatives (Col 3:23).

We should be driven daily to fulfill His desires because our motivation is that we have God's promise that our work "is not in vain." It is the Lord Jesus Christ we are serving and responsible to daily." Remember that the Lord will give you an inheritance as your reward, and that the Master you are serving is Christ. But if you do what is wrong, you will be paid back for the wrong you have done. For God has no favorites. (Col 3:24–25)

We cannot pick various scriptures out of His word to meet our comfort level and a life of convenience. The book of James illustrates that one who indeed professes to trust the Lord does not cling to the world and its vanity, but they are cemented in His Word and its value—for it is priceless to live it, proclaim it, and share it daily.

> James 2:14–17, "What good is it, dear brothers, and sisters if you say you have faith but don't show it by your actions? Can that kind of faith save anyone? Suppose you see a brother or sister who has no food or clothing, and you say, "Goodbye and have a good day; stay warm and eat well,"—but then you don't give that person any food or clothing. What good does that do? So, you see, faith by itself isn't enough. Unless it produces good deeds, it is dead and useless."

CHAPTER 19

Godly Cleansing

Num 19:11–13, "All those who touch a dead human body will be ceremonially unclean for seven days. They must purify themselves on the third and seventh days with the water of purification; then, they will be purified. But if they do not do this on the third and seventh days, they will continue to be unclean even after the seventh day. All those who touch a dead body and do not purify themselves in the proper way defile the LORD's Tabernacle, and they will be cut off from the community of Israel. Since the water of purification was not sprinkled on them, their defilement continues."

Death was the strongest of corruption because it was the final result of sin. One that was ceremonially unclean meant they were "excluded from the fellowship and worship of God, plus the fellowship of God's people. What a feeling of isolation to know that you cannot be with your Lord and fellow believers." It was a severe offense if a defiled person refused to be purified because defiled people corrupted the camp.

God's presence dwelt in the Tabernacle, and He walked among the people; therefore, the camp had to be kept holy. One who was unclean needed purification. And here's the key takeaway—"they could not ignore their condition." They were still part of the nation—unless they refused to address their unclean condition. They needed to understand that unclean people "who refused to be cleansed" were cut off from the nation (Num 19:20) and stoned to death.

Cleanliness, both ritual and actual, was fundamental to establishing and preserving holiness throughout the Israelite community. Examples:

Circumcision, handwashing, foot washing, bathing, and baptism are some of the many purification practices found in Scripture. The acts of washing and cleansing rituals served as ways to be freed from curses and guilt for wrongdoing. Many of us have heard this saying, "Cleanliness is next to godliness," which may have originated from John Wesley because he often emphasized the importance of spiritual cleanliness in his sermons.

While the exact phrase is not found in God's word, the concept is clearly expressed in its underlying message. Actual and spiritual purification and cleansings were featured prominently in Old Testament Jewish ceremonial rituals. For the Hebrew people, cleanliness wasn't "next to godliness" —because God's standards for the Israelites touched on every aspect of their lives.

A Holy God established these rites to show sinners how to be cleansed from their iniquities and reconciled to God. Ritual purification was essential in Israelite worship because God required His people to be a pure and holy nation (Exod 19:6).

For the Jews, holiness had to be reflected in how they lived, prioritizing the moral and spiritual virtues God revealed in His laws. He wanted them to live out His holy attributes so He would be glorified and not the ways of man. Unlike all the other nations, God had given his people specific guidelines concerning hygiene and cleanliness. He showed them how to maintain purity and what to do to regain it if they lost it through carelessness or disobedience.[1]

As believers today, we must remember that even those the law was relevant to all of Israel, especially to the priests, because they had the potential to defile the Tabernacle of the LORD—under the New Covenant, the Christian also has a special call to purity because an impure believer may violate the dwelling place of God (1 Cor 6:19–20). The great theologian Charles Spurgeon said, "The feet want constant washing. The daily defilement of our daily walk through an ungodly world brings upon us the daily necessity of being cleaned from fresh sin and that the mighty Master supplies to us."[2]

Jesus tells us in the Gospel of John chapter thirteen," Unless I wash you, you won't belong to Me; a person who has bathed all over does not need to wash, except for the feet, to be entirely clean. And you disciples are clean, but not all of you." Our Lord knows if we're spiritually pure or not, for He knew that there would be one amongst them that would share food with the Lord, but he was not wholly right with Him.

While this passage is an example of a servant's attitude, it comes down to a person's "willingness to submit, be humble and come clean," for without this step, there will be no growth. Water throughout the New Testament is "a

1. Fairchild, "Cleanliness is Next to Godliness and the Bible."
2. "Numbers 19—The Red Heifer and The Cleansing Waters."

symbol of our spiritual cleansing." Without that spiritual cleansing, our life has no justification or sanctification. Jesus emphasized the importance of repentance and spiritual renewal—for we need the "Living Water," and that is Christ revealed in our life through the power of His Spirit.

In today's swarm of unrighteousness, we can so easily get sucked into the storms of impurity and unholy waters because our flesh is so weak! Sometimes, we must submit our whole lives, externally and internally, into God's caring hands. We must go through all the detox stages to remove the filthiness and ugliness of our godless behavior in our daily lives. So often, we must go through the spiritual exercises of extracting all those dirty toxins from our inner being so we can portray a life outwardly that is more pleasing to Him.

This is vital because we can never attain righteousness and, for sure, holiness when we succumb to the poisonous life that is permeating this world. So, whether it's a bad habit, continual behavior that is godless, ungracious and hateful words spewing from our mouth like a nasty firehose, an unfiltered mind, or a fleshly eye-glazing life full of lust, pride, and greed, it's time to come clean—because "death to sin always leads to life and freedom."

Our Loving and Faithful God can rehabilitate anyone 24-7 365 for the rest of our time on this Earth. It's available for anyone willing and able to come to Him with a genuine, humble, and repentant heart. A spiritual cleansing session may be challenging at the time, but in the long run, it will enable us to hear the Spirit's voice clearly so we can apply the power of God's word to our lives.

This triumphant stage will lead to heights of praise, thanksgiving, fellowship, and sweet worship to our Lord. That moment when the flesh is being removed will seem intense because we're so attached to it. But no matter the torment we may feel in that moment, by the power of His grace, we can press on in life (2 Cor 12:9). This is critical because a prize awaits us that will bring us such joy and excitement. We will see the benefits of pursuing His purity and righteousness as we walk in the steps of our Lord and Savior.

> 1 John 1:7–9, "But if we are living in the light, as God is in the light, then we have fellowship with each other, and the blood of Jesus, his Son, cleanses us from all sin. If we claim we have no sin, we are only fooling ourselves and not living in the truth. But if we confess our sins to him, he is faithful and just to forgive us our sins and to cleanse us from all wickedness."

CHAPTER 20

Godly Response

Num 20:1–8, "In the first month of the year, the whole community of Israel arrived in the wilderness of Zin and camped at Kadesh. While they were there, Miriam died and was buried. There was no water for the people to drink at that place, so they rebelled against Moses and Aaron. The people blamed Moses and said, "If only we had died in the LORD's presence with our brothers! Why have you brought the congregation of the LORD's people into this wilderness to die, along with all our livestock? Why did you make us leave Egypt and bring us here to this terrible place? This land has no grain, no figs, no grapes, no pomegranates, and no water to drink!" Moses and Aaron turned away from the people and went to the entrance of the Tabernacle, where they fell face down on the ground. Then the glorious presence of the LORD appeared to them, and the LORD said to Moses, "You and Aaron must take the staff and assemble the entire community. As the people watch, speak to the rock over there, and it will pour out its water. You will provide enough water from the rock to satisfy the whole community and their livestock." And we know the rest of this story!

In chapter twenty, we are very familiar with Moses's striking of the rock—when God told him to speak to the rock, and it would pour out water, but Moses did not respond the way God told Him. In his haste, he reacted by not speaking to the rock like God commanded, but he struck it not once but twice, which would cost him dearly.

Before we look at Moses' flaw, I want to touch on the people who were reacting in ungodly ways with all their murmuring, complaining, and whining. Why? Because the most precious commodities to them for survival were not available, and once again, their mistrust in God's provision would lead to their sinful acts.

After approximately thirty-seven years in the wilderness, it was apparent this generation of Israelites forgot the reason for their years of wandering in that barren land, which resulted from their parent's rebellion and disobedience, as well as their own sins. It seems they were not holding themselves accountable for their defiant ways, so what do they do? They go after Moses and Aaron.

But I love what Moses and Aaron did at this point, even though they are built up with frustration "to no end." They turned away from the people, went into the presence of Almighty God, and fell face down on the ground—and with that type of response, what happened? God came forward!

Their godly response by approaching God and falling before Him first is due to their faith in Him alone. What a beautiful picture for us to follow when confronted with the fiery arrows of attack against us; we can go to God anytime. He wants us to respond to Him first before we allow our emotions to get out of line.

Always remember, God knows our hearts, real motives, and true desires, but most importantly, He knows who will respond to Him first when various circumstances are getting the best of us. He always wants us to come to Him when we need His aid in life's most critical stages. When the moment and time are right, and we may be at our wit's end—God will break through all our barriers and struggles, and the inward call of God's Spirit becomes irresistible. And those believers who are abiding in Him will respond and come to Him first—because it's not in us, as His children, to reject the help of the Lord.

But if we're too busy, we may not hear or heed His call because if we're too caught up in our own ways, we may ignore it, and pride may prevent us from hearing His voice. Sometimes it may take something tragic in our lives where He will get our attention because He knows how to get us to fall to our knees in absolute fear and reverence to the One who can supply our every need. So often, we need a lesson in humility to help us realize our need to fall before Him. But our Sovereign God also knows when we ignore Him and do the opposite of His word and commands.

When God told Moses to "speak to the rock," Moses 'struck it.' And when he did not trust God enough to demonstrate His holiness to the people of Israel, this prevented Moses from leading God's children into the land God had promised. Moses obeyed God initially but went astray—in that one act.

Was Moses so angry and frustrated with the Israelites that He forgot what God instructed him? Or was Moses habitually doing what he did back in Exodus chapter seventeen, where God told Moses to strike the rock once, but here he struck it twice? Was Moses' haste reaction due to his possibility of being at his wit's end? God told Moses to do "one" thing: "Speak to the rock, and water will pour out."

So simple and straightforward, but Moses added his own method to the madness, and this one act of disobedience led to this, "Moses would never lead the people into the Promise Land!" He would see it from afar, and that's it! But here's an amazing point even though Moses did not obey God completely—water still poured from the rock. God could have made a fool of Moses, but He still provided for them through it all!

God's word tells us in Phil 4:19 that He will provide "all" our needs according to His riches in glory in Jesus Christ. God is an awesome Provider, and too often, regardless of our ignorance! When God said that He would take the Israelites as His own and that I will be your God regardless of all the ugliness in their lives and even Moses' disobedience—God's providence is unmatched! Our Lord wants to help, develop, strengthen, guide, and comfort us—because He wants to "be with us" through it all!

His Holy word and Spirit are ever present through all our troubles, even when we get out of line and react out of the flesh versus responding from the spirit. We don't deserve His mercy when we allow our flesh to get the best of us! But in all His ways, He is always there for us—no matter what. When we respond to God in the right way, it leaves the open door of communication to hear Him, know Him and grow closer to Him, and better understand life today, tomorrow, and in the future.

> Jer 33:3, "Ask me, and I will tell you remarkable secrets you do not know about things to come."

> Ps 50:15, "Then call on me when you are in trouble, and I will rescue you, and you will give me glory."

> Ps 145:18–20, "The LORD is close to all who call on him, yes, to all who call on him in truth. He grants the desires of those who fear him; he hears their cries for help and rescues them. The LORD protects all those who love him, but he destroys the wicked."

CHAPTER 21

Godly Symbol

Num 21:4–9, "Then the people of Israel set out from Mount Hor, taking the road to the Red Sea to go around the land of Edom. But the people grew impatient with the long journey and began to speak against God and Moses. "Why have you brought us out of Egypt to die here in the wilderness?" they complained. "There is nothing to eat here and nothing to drink. And we hate this horrible manna!" So, the LORD sent poisonous snakes among the people, and many were bitten and died. Then the people came to Moses and cried out, "We have sinned by speaking against the LORD and against you. Pray that the LORD will take away the snakes." So, Moses prayed for the people. Then the LORD told him, "Make a replica of a poisonous snake and attach it to a pole. All who are bitten will live if they simply look at it!" So, Moses made a snake out of bronze and attached it to a pole. Then anyone who was bitten by a snake could look at the bronze snake and be healed!"

An excellent reference to the reasons for God's children continuous complaining is found in Psalm chapter seventy-eight, where we see: "Their spirits were consistently unfaithful to God, and they were disobedient and disregarded God's laws and commands." When the roots of rebellion run deep, they start to compound and can lead anyone to resist and refuse the ways of God.

Because once again, the Israelites complained, and God's protection ceased at this point because of their continuous grumbling. This would lead God to send poisonous snakes to bite and kill, where many of the original generation who were freed and witnessed all of God's miracles would die. And now, we're going to see a profound move from God that would lay out a powerful prophecy for the future of man and line up with one of the most memorable passages in God's word.

In the Bible, we see times when God used poisonous snakes to punish the people for their unbelief in Him and constant complaining. In their journey through the wilderness, various types of snakes hid and would often attack without warning—sound familiar? The Israelites greatly feared the snakes because they knew one bite would eventually lead to a slow death and often severe suffering. All because of their habitual acts of ignorance.

Spurgeon said, "When the grumbling humor is on us, we complain of anything and everything, as did these Israelites: they complained of God, they complained of Moses; they complained of the manna. They would have been ready to complain of Aaron; fortunately for him, he had been dead a month or so, so they poured more gall upon Moses. To men in this state, nothing is right: nothing can be right."

When you look at this passage, it was a discouraging situation but an opportunity for God's children to trust Him in all His ways. The same God who gave them victory at Hormah at the beginning of this chapter and provided all their needs would also guide them through this setback.[1]

Why would God use a bronze serpent hoisted on a pole as a means of life if they looked upon this replica? The serpent is a picture of evil, and bronze is associated with judgment, which depicts evil being judged. They did not have to do anything but look at the serpent on the pole and trust in God's most divine ways, and they would be saved.

Some probably thought it was foolish to look at this serpent on a hoisted pole as a means of life, but if they failed to obey God, they would perish because of their unbelief. Then there were those who looked at that symbol on the pole, remembering their sinful ways and probably realized they should have been bitten and deserved to die. But God's mercy is boundless, His love is immeasurable, and His grace is priceless! It was not the snake that would heal them, but belief in God's word when He said, "Look at it."

God would heal them if they simply believed in His command, demonstrating their obedience to His instructions. So often in life, maybe we need the view of a Christian symbol of faith to help us remember all of God's provisions and protection so our flesh will not fall prey to a grumbling state.

God has placed His symbols of Christianity and Faith in view as reminders for us today. Such as:

- The Cross represents Christ's victory over sin and death through the sacrifice of his own body on the cross.

---

1. "Numbers 21—On the Way to Canaan."

- The Christian Fish identified early Christians as followers of Jesus Christ and expressed their affinity to Christianity.

- The Christian Dove represents the Holy Spirit or Holy Ghost in Christianity.

- The Crown of Thorns, in the Bible, often represents sin, and therefore, the crown of thorns is fitting—because Jesus would bear the sins of the world. But a crown is also appropriate because it represents the suffering King of Christianity—Jesus Christ, our King of kings and Lord of lords.

- The Trinity represents the belief that God is one Being made up of three distinct Persons who exist in co-equal and co-eternal communion as the Father, Son, and Holy Spirit.

- The Light or Candle, when Jesus spoke again to the people, he said, "I am the light of the world." Light represents the presence of God in our lives.

- The Christian Star, while predominately recognized as a symbol of Judaism and Israel, many Christians also identify with the Star of David.

- Bread and Wine, which represent the Lord's Supper or Communion. While bread symbolizes life and nourishes life, wine represents God's covenant in blood, poured out in payment for mankind's sin.

- The Rainbow symbolizes God's faithfulness and promise never to destroy the Earth by flood again.

- The Christian Circle is the unending circle or wedding ring, which symbolizes eternity. For Christian couples, exchanging is the outward expression of the inward bond, as two hearts unite as one and promise to love each other with fidelity for all their lives. Likewise, the wedding covenant and the husband-and-wife relationship is a picture of the relationship between Jesus Christ and his bride, the church.

- The Lamb of God, which represents Jesus Christ, is the perfect, sinless sacrifice God offers to atone for man's sins.

- The Holy Bible is God's infallible and inerrant Word. It is the Christian's handbook for life. It's God's message of love, mercy, and grace to mankind. All Scripture is God-breathed and is useful for teaching, rebuking, correcting, and training in righteousness.

- The Ten Commandment Tablets are the Laws of God given to the people of Israel through Moses after leading them out of Egypt. They offer basic rules of behavior for spiritual and moral living.

- The Crown and Cross is a familiar symbol in Christian churches. It represents the reward awaiting in Heaven (the crown) that believers will receive after the suffering and trials of life on Earth (the cross).

- Alpha and Omega, together these two letters form a monogram or symbol for one of the names of Jesus Christ, meaning "the Beginning and the End."

These marks of our Christian faith should always remind us of our Heavenly Creator and Whom we aim to symbolize in our everyday life—Jesus Christ. Even many symbols of healing in the field of medicine took birth from this passage in Numbers chapter twenty-one, so why can't we, as followers of Christ, represent Him in these figures?

This spiritual and everlasting story hinges upon this in John 3:14–16: "*And as Moses lifted up the serpent in the wilderness, even so, must the Son of Man be lifted up, that whoever believes in Him should not perish but have eternal life. And in verse sixteen, one of the most memorized passages in all of God's word, "For God so loved the world that He gave His only begotten son for whosoever believes in Him will not perish but have eternal life.*"

When we view our lives through the cross, we see ourselves the way God wants to see us, as those who symbolize the representatives of Jesus Christ while on this earth. As Hebrews chapter two reminds us, we must always keep our eyes upon Jesus Christ—the Champion of Life—Who initiates and perfects our faith, endured the cross for our sins, and disregards the shame that the Old Rugged Cross brought because that's how much He loves us.

> 1 Peter 2:24, "He personally carried our sins in his body on the cross so that we can be dead to sin and live for what is right. By his wounds, you are healed."

Personal Comment: I cannot count the times when I traveled to a major city or a small town where you would see signs outside their city limits signifying the importance of their community. For example, many cities and especially small towns will not hesitate one minute to place a billboard outside their community, letting the world know that a famous person is from their little town. Or if you go to a city like Las Vegas and New York, you will get a strong sense of what you're about to enter with the type of signs they promote and are very proud of. Many communities in the United States seem very proud of their hometown celebrities. Wouldn't it be wonderful if every town and city across this country had a billboard outside their city limits that planted seeds of salvation with the image of our Lord?

CHAPTER 22

God Engages

Num 22:21–23, 28–31, "So, the next morning, Balaam got up, saddled his donkey, and started off with the Moabite officials. But God was angry that Balaam was going, so he sent the angel of the LORD to stand in the road to block his way. As Balaam and two servants were riding along, Balaam's donkey saw the angel of the LORD standing in the road with a drawn sword in his hand. The donkey bolted off the road into a field, but Balaam beat it and turned it back onto the road. Then the LORD gave the donkey the ability to speak. "What have I done to you that deserves your beating me three times?" it asked Balaam. "You have made me look like a fool!" Balaam shouted. "If I had a sword with me, I would kill you!" "But I am the same donkey you have ridden all your life," the donkey answered. "Have I ever done anything like this before? "No," Balaam admitted. Then the LORD opened Balaam's eyes, and he saw the angel of the LORD standing in the roadway with a drawn sword in his hand. Balaam bowed his head and fell face down on the ground before him."

Earlier in this chapter, we see Balaam was a sorcerer, a diviner, and a man who was called to place curses and even blessings on others. Although he was a wicked prophet, he was not a false prophet because Balaam heard from God and gave him some accurate prophecies to speak. However, Balaam's heart was not right with God, and eventually, he showed his true colors by betraying Israel and leading them astray. As a result, he was known throughout the land as a man who could manipulate gods, but not the Almighty and Sovereign God.

Balaam was half-hearted towards the Lord and the other half towards his own worldly ways. Balaam had "some" knowledge of God, but he was weak in the flesh because he still could not abandon his wicked ways; he was so full of greed and was known by many for using his position and gifts for money. So why would God use a misguided prophet like Balaam in this amazing story? Because God wanted to get a message to Moab—and Balaam was available. Just like Pharaoh, God can use wicked and evil people available at the right place and time for His purpose, plan, and glory!

As we look at the passage above, you must admit that this character, Balaam, was placed in God's word to teach us a lesson. A man with wrong intentions was spoken about almost sixty times and in eight books of the bible—more than the Apostles and Mary, the mother of Jesus. So, what's the point here?

From the get-go, Balaam's off to a bad start because God is angry with him because of his greedy attitude. His "wrong" motives were the underlying reason for his actions (Prov 16:2). Maybe God inserted Balaam's example so many times for us in His word because, too often in life, our motives and desires are not entirely in line with His will and plan. And maybe we are not listening to His voice so He can direct us correctly in our everyday lives.

In this story, the donkey sees the angel of God, but Balaam doesn't. First, God gives the donkey the ability to speak; and amazingly, Balaam converses with the donkey. And then, out of the words from Balaam's mouth, he admits that this creature "has never done anything like this before to get his attention and save him." Then God opened Balaam's eyes so he could now see the angel of the Lord—and it humbled Balaam to his hands and knees.

Yes, the donkey saved Balaam's life and, at the same time, made Balaam look foolish in more ways than one. Donkeys were very dependable animals in all facets of use, which may explain why Balaam became so angry when his donkey refused to obey him and move, so he lashed out at the donkey. Was God using this illustration for us today? Have you ever blamed someone else who was innocent of something—when come to find out—it was an underlying issue with you?

The doctrine of Balaam is the attitude that one can cooperate with the world and still serve God; while we know Jesus instructs us, we cannot serve two masters. This false belief teaches compromise, "wanting Christians to forget" that they are called to be separate and holy and not the ways of the world. When we depict an outward appearance of obeying God, but our hearts are hard or not in line with Him, God knows—as He did with Balaam.

If we get caught up in this state of hypocrisy, then we are deceiving ourselves and others, and we, too, can become like Balaam since he was a manipulator and user. God's word tells us in Rev 2:14, in Christ's letter to the church of Pergamum, "But I have a few complaints against you. You tolerate some among you whose teaching is like that of Balaam, who showed Balak how to trip up the people of Israel. He taught them to sin by eating food offered to idols and committing sexual sin." In other words, he was a stumbling block to the children of Israel because he encouraged God's children to worship idols.

This false doctrine of Balaam is the view that Christians can—or even should—compromise their convictions for the sake of popularity, money, self-gratification, or personal gain. It's the attitude that treats sin as "no big deal." While Christians can't—and shouldn't shun sinners or unbelievers (1 Cor 5:9–13), we must stand up for the truth (Eph 4:25), righteousness (Prov 23:20; Rom 14:22), and goodness (2 Pet 1:5, Matt 5:16).

No matter what others want to hear, we must always be faithful to the Gospel (John 4:16–18; 8:11; Acts 24:24–25). That is our Christian duty because a wholehearted believer and follower of Jesus Christ is always available to do His will, fulfill His purpose and plan, and serve when and where needed for His glory.[1] This is going to be a gut-punch but as the inmates used to say in the prison, as a Christian, "*You're either all in or not in at all!* We cannot be like Balaam and be half-hearted!

God gets involved in our lives to ensure that His true children use all their God-given gifts genuinely for His glory while exhibiting the Fruit of the Spirit (Gal 5:22–23). There's no fabricated, mystical, or magical formula for using His gifts because His Spirit teaches and guides us in all His ways. And when they're in use at just the right time and place, you could be a blessing in someone's life who desperately needed it. God is Omnipresent and will step in when needed and use an authentic heart at just the right time to get His message to someone you care for and needs the Lord.

And even for many of us today, there will be times when God will take part in our lives, and He will employ gifted Christians (like a donkey) to show us our own err. There will be words of wisdom through that person from God, but it's our choice to submit to humility and see the righteous ways of the Lord.

Remember that our God is Sovereign, and He directs our steps and laces them together with His plans for you and me, Jeremiah 29:11–13. He does not neglect us in His plans or leave us to our own devices. He is so intricately and powerfully engaged where He will bring us to that point in our lives—when He wants, as He did with Jonah.

> Rom 8:15–17. "So, you have not received a spirit that makes you fearful slaves. Instead, you received God's Spirit when he adopted you as his own children. Now we call him "Abba, Father." His Spirit joins with our spirit to affirm that we are God's children. And since we are his children, we are his heirs. Together with Christ, we are heirs of God's glory. But if we are to share his glory, we must also share his suffering."

1. "The Doctrine of Balaam."

CHAPTER 23

God's Protection

Num 23:1–12, "Then Balaam said to King Balak, "Build me seven altars here, and prepare seven young bulls and seven rams for me to sacrifice." Balak followed his instructions, and the two of them sacrificed a young bull and a ram on each altar. Then Balaam said to Balak, "Stand here by your burnt offerings, and I will go to see if the Lord will respond to me. Then I will tell you whatever he reveals to me." So, Balaam went alone to the top of a bare hill, and God met him there. Balaam said to him, "I have prepared seven altars and have sacrificed a young bull and a ram on each altar."

"The Lord gave Balaam a message for King Balak. Then he said, "Go back to Balak and give him my message." So, Balaam returned and found the king standing beside his burnt offerings with all the officials of Moab. This was the message Balaam delivered: "Balak summoned me to come from Aram; the king of Moab brought me from the eastern hills. 'Come,' he said, 'curse Jacob for me! Come and announce Israel's doom.' But how can I curse those whom God has not cursed? How can I condemn those whom the Lord has not condemned? I see them from the clifftops; I watch them from the hills. I see a people who live by themselves, set apart from other nations. Who can count Jacob's descendants as numerous as dust? Who can count even a fourth of Israel's people? Let me die like the righteous; let my life end like theirs."

"Then King Balak demanded of Balaam, "What have you done to me? I brought you to curse my enemies. Instead, you have blessed them!" But Balaam replied, *"I will speak only the message that the Lord puts in my mouth."*

The last statement in this passage is powerful; even from a wicked prophet and conniver like Balaam! "I will speak only the message that the Lord puts in my mouth." Regardless of the pressures in life to conform to the ways of our family heritage or the practices of society and culture, do we act and speak "exactly" to what God commands us to do? Or do we cave in and compromise to our comfort zone? No matter the situation or surrounding environment, do we adhere to every breath of His word daily?

God never told Balaam to build an altar to Him, much less seven altars with seven sacrifices in seven different high places. These seven altars and burnt offerings were Balaam and Balak's ideas, not God's. Balaam no doubt wanted seven altars, seven bulls, and seven rams to offer upon those seven altars because he saw the significance of the number seven. Believing that he was having Balak set up the perfect and complete system for appealing to God, he thought he might change His mind regarding cursing Israel.

Even a corrupt prophet like Balaam, who was not wholeheartedly dedicated to the Lord, somehow knew to build seven altars in seven different places. What is so striking about this is that the number seven is a holy number that often represents completion or divine fulfillment. God has used seven multiple times throughout Scripture. Balak, a heathen, may have thought that these altars were being erected in honor of Baal, but it is evident from Numbers 23:4 that they were prepared for the worship of the One True God. Undoubtedly, God's Almighty hands were upon His children throughout this story working out His plan through godless people.

Because the powerful takeaway for us in this passage is the absolute protection of God for His nation. In verse eight, God tells Balaam to tell Balak this, "But how can I curse those whom God has not cursed? How can I condemn those whom the Lord has not condemned?" This is the first time Balaam specifically tells Balak that he cannot curse Israel because God had not cursed His own children, which tells us that any all-out attempts by evil men to curse God's people will be futile.

The fundamental meaning of this declaration is that since God has not cursed His own, Balaam sure does not have the power to do so. Blessed are the ones the Lord himself will not curse, "but instead He will pronounce His blessings upon them." Wow! This is the privilege of all the children of God and every single believer in Jesus Christ. To every secret or open enemy conspiring and concocting their plan against God's people, the Lord says, "Thou shalt not curse whom I have blessed." Amen!

God promised physical protection to His people, the Israelites, as they kept the law (Deut 7:11–26). And that divine protection extended to keep them safe against the nations coming against them as they entered the Promise

Land. God's word stands true when He says that He will protect us. In times of physical and spiritual attack and threatening situations, those who trust the Lord find Him a strong Protector and Provider. "He shields all who take refuge in him" (Ps 18:30).

In the book of Psalm, God's word reminds us that His protection is amid all our dangers. While God doesn't promise any of us a world free from danger, He promises us He will help us when we face the dangers of this world. Psalm chapter 91 tells us, "Those who live in the shelter of the Most-High will find rest in the shadow of the Almighty. This I declare about the Lord: He alone is my refuge, my place of safety; he is my God, and I trust him. For he will rescue you from every trap and protect you from deadly diseases and will cover you with his feathers. He will shelter you with his wings. His faithful promises are your armor and protection. Do not be afraid of the terrors of the night, nor the arrow that flies in the day. Do not dread the disease that stalks in darkness, nor the disaster that strikes at midday. Though a thousand fall at your side, though ten thousand are dying around you, these evils will not touch you. Just open your eyes and see how the wicked are punished. If you make the Lord your refuge, if you make the Most-High your shelter, no evil will conquer you; no plague will come near your home. For he will order his angels to protect you wherever you go."

In today's crazy and tumultuous times, many have fears that can rattle our spiritual cages. While some may feel that David wrote this Psalm because it contains some of his language of "strongholds and shields," which reminds us of David crying out to the Lord so often for protection, this chapter has no title. This leads many scholars to say that the author is unknown. I believe God leaves some chapters untitled and anonymous, so we don't get so focused on the person but on the context of His message.

Also, in this profound chapter, we see a portrait of the importance of absolute trust in our Lord. In times of intense torment and anxiety, we should swap in all our fear-mongering ways and rely upon the One Who has always seen us through the storms of life. They should not be spiritually blind to us, for those little victories in our life are reminders of His presence and protection. Sometimes, we need to sit back and put His ways into perspective.

The PowerPoint is that when we live and rest in Him, we're entirely entrusting our lives to His protective Hands, and in return, we're committing and pledging our daily devotion to Him. When we do this, we will know beyond a shadow of a doubt, He has our back, and we will be safe in the end.

Charles Spurgeon, the great theologian, said this about Psalm 91, "In the whole collection there is not a more cheering Psalms, its tone is elevated and sustained throughout, faith is at its best, and speaks nobly." "It is one of the most excellent works of this kind that has ever appeared. It is impossible to imagine anything more solid, more beautiful, more profound, or more ornamented."

In all times of distress, we should humbly pray to our Lord for His protection, but most importantly, we should expect it. And during our exceptional times of fear, God may lead us down an alternative path, but always know it's for our good. Therefore, we should always trust Him through it all, praying for His will to be done and that He's glorified. No matter our situations in life, we must continually ask Him for trust, wisdom, discernment, understanding, guidance, courage, boldness, strength, peace, comfort, and His joy!

Remember this: God's promise of protection does not guarantee that we will never know pain, loss, or suffering—look at the story of Job. Yes, God can deliver us from any physical calamity or trouble, but His will may not be to do so. Sometimes He uses these times of trial to purify us for something much better. And during these times, we should "count it pure joy" because, by allowing trials, God tests our faith to develop more profound confidence so that we persevere and grow to maturity and Christlikeness (James 1:2–3).

Protecting us from trials is not always beneficial because we can become too relaxed and comfortable in our earthly life and focus on the wrong type of joy. God's word reminds us in Neh 8:10, "The joy of the Lord is our strength," and this is brought to fullness when we accept His provision of righteousness by grace that reunites us so we can enjoy His presence and protection.

Our joy and strength will progressively increase when we focus on God's constant presence and promises. But our joy and strength will also decrease if we focus on flawed, weak, and undependable people and the uncertain circumstances in our lives. God intends for you and me to be Christlike students of His word where our faith is steadfast in His protective hands until our day of glory!

> Rom 14:17–19, "For the Kingdom of God is not a matter of what we eat or drink, but of living a life of goodness and peace and joy in the Holy Spirit. If you serve Christ with this attitude, you will please God, and others will approve of you, too. So then, let us aim for harmony in the church and try to build each other up."

CHAPTER 24

Godly Ambitions

Num 24: 10–13, "King Balak flew into a rage against Balaam. He angrily clapped his hands and shouted, "I called you to curse my enemies! Instead, you have blessed them three times. Now get out of here! Go back home! I promised to reward you richly, but the LORD has kept you from your reward." Balaam told Balak, "Don't you remember what I told your messengers? I said, 'Even if Balak were to give me his palace filled with silver and gold, I would be powerless to do anything against the will of the LORD.' I told you that I could say only what the LORD says!"

By now, we know of Balaam's past—he was a sorcerer and often looked for omens or other signs to help him in foretelling the future. However, at the beginning of chapter twenty-four, in this compelling situation, it is clear that Almighty God has influenced Balaam. The scriptures tell us, "By now, Balaam realized that the LORD was determined to bless Israel, so he did not resort to divination as before." But in this storyline, we see the money used to hire Balaam was not well spent. Knowing this, Balak said that he would not pay Balaam.

There is a sense, which was confirmed, that the LORD had kept Balaam back from honor because his corrupt heart was more focused on money as a prophet versus a faithful servant of God. So, he would not receive any funds, which was the LORD's doing. Balaam knew he would not receive the reward he hoped for because he failed to please his employer (God). Perhaps at that moment, Balaam saw the greater wisdom of God in telling him not to go because now it seemed the whole trip was a big waste.[1] Remember this, a person not

---

1. "Numbers 24— The Prophecies of Balaam."

wholeheartedly devoted to God will always be slow in obtaining His wisdom, if at all.

But we cannot overlook Balak's persistent and crafty acts and attempts to get what he wanted. After two unsuccessful attempts to cause Balaam to curse Israel, Balak was still willing to try again. It is evident that Balak wanted these curses upon God's children so badly that we see his desperate acts of selfish measures. He probably thought it was just a matter of time before his persuasive ways and cunning words would eventually get him what he wanted. Balak thought another approach and angle would give him the desired results.

It never seems to amaze me that when a person is out for their own selfish ambitions, they will attempt all levels of shrewdness to get what they want out of life—at all costs. And so often, they are looking for the shortcut in life. Prov 11:18 reminds us, "Upright citizens are good for a city and make it prosper, but the talk of the wicked tears it apart." The parallels between the two stories suggest that Balak, like Balaam, blindly attempted to go against the Lord—because their evil desires consumed them.

Where the world teaches us to go all out and be the best we can be and live our best life now, or have a bigger house, nicer car, or simply more in life, the Bible teaches us the opposite: "Let nothing be done through selfish ambition or conceit, but in lowliness of mind let each esteem others better than himself" (Phil 2:3). The apostle Paul tells us, "So whether we are here in this body or away from this body, our goal is to please him" (2 Cor 5:9). God's word clearly tells us, that those who seek honor and esteem from men cannot believe in Jesus (Matthew 6:24; Romans 8:7; James 4:4). Those whose seek self-ambition and want to be popular with the world cannot be true, faithful servants of Jesus Christ.

We can learn from the story of Balaam and Balak that God knows our real motives and desires in life. We cannot take shortcuts to get what we want; God must be part of our daily steps and plan for life's course. When we don't include Him, He can and will get our attention—and it could be like a voice through a donkey—if He desires.

If we attempt ways of wickedness and not the ways of God, eventually, what will surface is our inability to hide our genuine hearts from God because He knows all! God's word reminds us in 2 Pet 2:15, "They have wandered off the right road and followed the footsteps of Balaam, son of Beor, who loved to earn money by doing wrong. But Balaam was stopped from his mad course when his donkey rebuked him with a human voice."

Balaam was hired by a pagan king (Balak), intending to curse Israel, God's nation. In Numbers, chapters 22–24, we discover that Balaam did what God told him for a while, but his absolute ambition and love for money would win—over time. In this second chapter of Peter's second epistle, the theme is entitled "Danger to growing Christians," for false teachers and wicked people are conspiring their own acts all around us, deceiving and tricking us with their sly words that woo us into an ungodly world of evil.

And just like these false teachers during Peter's days, Balaam also used religion for his personal advancement, a sin God takes seriously. In this story of Balak and Balaam, we also see the danger of enticing others in sinful ways because it will not end well. Remember, whatever voice we lean to more in life will determine our outcome—it could lead to blessings or curses.

When seeking to hear from the Lord, we must ensure that it's His voice and not our own thoughts —or someone else's idea that could be misleading and misguiding. God's voice is consistent with His Word and leads us toward righteous ambitions. He speaks to our hearts through His Holy Spirit compellingly because it always leads to His Truths. The more we lean in with discerning ears, the easier it is to hear His voice. Just like listening to a close friend in those most sincere and precious moments, we heed their voice because we trust them and long to hear their words of wisdom. So, what is our automatic response? We get still and listen consciously. Why?

It's because we know them and have that close-knit relationship. We believe in their advice because we know they have our best interest at heart—it's like their conscience is in sync with our every move and thought. It's mainly because of a longstanding bond that you've had for years with that person. Their voice and words are like clockwork, always consistent and timely. Doesn't this describe the type of bond we should have with God so that we can know for sure it's His voice and we're attaining a clear path of godly ambitions that will not lead to destruction?

> Rom 10:17, "So faith comes from hearing, and that is hearing the Good News about Christ."

> John 10:27, "My sheep listen to my voice; I know them, and they follow me."

> John 8:47, "Anyone who belongs to God listens gladly to the words of God. But you don't listen because you don't belong to God."

It is so vital that we differentiate between the falsehoods of this world and the voice of God. We can only stay on the right course of godly ambitions when we're in tune with the inerrancy of God's word and His Spirit. In John 8:47, this passage tells us that if we don't have spiritual eyes to see, righteous ears to hear, a renewed spirit of the mind, and discerning hearts to understand, we will not hear the words of God, which means we are not of God. So, get in tune with His voice; it's imperative for our well-being.

CHAPTER 25

Godless Match

Num 25:1–3, "While the Israelites were camped at Acacia Grove, some of the men defiled themselves by having sexual relations with local Moabite women. These women invited them to attend sacrifices to their gods, so the Israelites feasted with them and worshiped the gods of Moab. In this way, Israel joined in the worship of Baal of Peor, causing the LORD's anger to blaze against his people."

The Moabites are neighbors to the Israelites and have found an effective way to corrupt God's chosen ones, thanks to the stumbling blocks Balaam put forth in all his selfish and wicked practices! If not through war and witchcraft, they discovered that the lure of sexual immorality and idolatry was their weakness. At first, the Israelites were not focused on worshipping idols; they were just interested in sex. And like so many, their one sin of lust for sexual immorality became a domino effect and led to more sins, and all of a sudden, they are in over their heads. Before long, their lust for sex led to them attending local feasts and celebrations involving idolatry, which was their demise.

Baal was known to be the most popular god in Canaan, which was the land God's children were about to enter. And unfortunately, the Israelites were continually attracted to Baal worship, where prostitution played a large part in the pagan lifestyle. Balaam, who just blessed the nation of Israel, is now the influencer who would mislead them into a world that fueled God's anger.

The Israelites, over time, would realize that Balaam's original concerns were not in their best interest, and his pagan ways led them astray. Their neighboring enemy could never accomplish what the Israelites did to themselves, for their sin and rebellion against the Lord were often their failings.

Their godless intentions did not require the enemy's help because they were masters of self-imposing evil upon themselves, easily led astray because they were not committed to God 100%! Christians today must be cautious and not self-inflict unspiritual acts into their lives, for they will lead us far away from God's will; if we're not close to His purpose and plan.

There are Balaam's all around us today (as we discovered his true character in chapters 22–24). We must have a discerning spirit to diagnose the words and deeds of those who are "supposedly" offering help. A key to our thrive for daily sanctification is based on our spiritual growth, values, and purpose. Paul reminds us in 2 Cor chapter 6:14–15 that if we're unequally yoked, we will be mismatched, going the opposite direction, "Don't team up with those who are unbelievers. How can righteousness be a partner with wickedness? How can light live with darkness? What harmony can there be between Christ and the devil? How can a believer be a partner with an unbeliever?"

Throughout the centuries, since the beginning of time, the enemy has been slithering his way into our lives with subtle whispers and inclinations to do things that we "should" know that are not of God. His cunning words have always been out to deceive us into following ungodly ways and not a Holy God. Our society and culture are filled with all types of godless paths, luring us down a road that is either false teachings or tempting ways of weakness that is out to snare us. If we're not strong in our faith and mix with others—"who are not on course with the Lord 100%", we will get pulled in the wrong direction.

This does not mean we avoid the unbelieving world "because they need the Lord!" But more than ever, we need discerning spirits so He can use us as His productive vessels. We cannot get vacuumed into the unbelieving world of paganism because if we're not "grounded" in all His Truths, we could get misled and off course. And then we've compromised ourselves to a world that offers no help and has no spiritual value!

The Corinth church was weak, for they were surrounded by idolatry and sexual immorality. And with these bombardments of temptation, they struggled with their Christian faith. Then false teachers and doctrine started to infiltrate the church and compounded the weakness of the Corinthian's trust in the Lord, which Paul reminded them of.

And then, to make matters worse, because their hearts and minds got distorted from the teachings of the Good News, they started to attack the very man who presented them with the "real truth" (Paul). This letter in Second Corinthians must have been challenging for Paul because they attacked his Christlike credentials. Once again, it's unfortunate that the enemy can so easily deceive us from the ways of the solid truth. Still, it's because we're not grounded in the firm foundation of God's doctrine, and we swiftly get sucked into the world of misguided principles.

A godless match for us as Christians is when we try to mix in or dabble with the principles of Satan, who governs the pagan, wicked, and unbelieving world. Christians should be separate from that type of world, just as Christ was separate from all the enemy's methods, purposes, and plans. He had no participation and formed no union with them. As mature Christians, we should know the difference between holy and unholy.

Attempting to live a Christian life with a non-Christian will only cause us to go around in circles in a state of confusion and chaos and never on a straight and righteous path. It is divisive where nothing but dissension exists. If Christ is to be the center of all relationships and the nucleus and motion of our daily Christian walk, where is the balance if the two are on different levels of belief? Because the scary thought is this; if we participate in a godless match and get immune to their lifestyle, spiritual blindness can set in, and then we're in dire trouble.

We must always remember that unbelievers have opposite worldviews and morals than Christians. If we're not careful, we can fall into the same traps as the Israelites did, and we can get a callous heart and become disobedient against the ways of God. The only way to ensure that you're either receiving godly advice and on His righteous path is to be a daily student of His word, which is the Way, Truth, and Life.

You can guarantee that you're on the right path by taking these steps: 1) Be Christlike by following the ways of Christ (1 Pet 2:21). 2) Be righteous and walk in the ways of the Spirit (Rom 8:4). 3) Show your love for Christ by obeying His word (John 14:15). 4) Walk by faith and not by sight (2 Cor 5:7). 5) Possess the attitude of Christ (Phil 2:5–11). 6) Exhibit Christlike qualities, (Gal 5;22–23, Eph 4:1–3). And 7) Be a living sacrifice and do not conform to the ways of the world, Rom (12:1–2).

But on the flip side, we are still to be a witness to the unbelieving world. Jesus reminds us in Matt 5:16, "In the same way, let your good deeds shine out for "all to see" so that everyone will praise your heavenly Father." And in 1 Pet 2:12, "Be careful to live properly among your unbelieving neighbors. Then even if they accuse you of doing wrong, they will see your honorable behavior and honor God when he judges the world."

However, if Christians conduct themselves no differently from the un-believing world, what good is our service? Suppose the unbelieving world is watching us with microscopes and scrutinizing every step of unrighteous-ness we take, and they see no difference between themselves and us as the

Christian community. What motivation will there be for them to forego their unbelieving lifestyle?

The unbeliever is already inherently hostile to the things of God, as the Bible reminds us in (1 Cor 2:14; Rom 8:7–8). If Christians conduct themselves as the unbelieving world does, then all we do is invite scorn and charges of hypocrisy. We must adhere to the truth of the Gospel so our godly words genuinely represent the Truth. Our ministry can either help the cause of Christ or hinder it. "Our ultimate aim is to match those of the godless world with a Holy God!" And that can only happen when we faithfully and obediently represent Christ in all His ways in our daily life!

> Ps 1:1–6, "Oh, the joys of those who do not follow the advice of the wicked, or stand around with sinners, or join in with mockers. But they delight in the law of the LORD, meditating on it day and night. They are like trees planted along the riverbank, bearing fruit each season. Their leaves never wither, and they prosper in all they do. But not the wicked! They are like worthless chaff scattered by the wind. They will be condemned at the time of judgment. Sinners will have no place among the godly. For the LORD watches over the path of the godly, but the path of the wicked leads to destruction."

CHAPTER 26

Second Chance

Num 26:1–4, "After the plague had ended, the Lord said to Moses and to Eleazar son of Aaron, the priest, "From the whole community of Israel, record the names of all the warriors by their families. List all the men twenty years old or older who are able to go to war." So, there on the plains of Moab beside the Jordan River, across from Jericho, Moses and Eleazar, the priest issued these instructions to the leaders of Israel: "List all the men of Israel twenty years old and older, just as the Lord commanded Moses."

The sin and rebellion against God forced Him to bring affliction and a plague upon the nation that would destroy twenty-four thousand Israelites in total. It could have been more if one man named Phinehas had not acted against those who rebelled against God. His "zeal (enthusiasm and devotion) for the Lord halted God's anger. "

This one man's faithfulness and stand for righteousness was why God stopped the angry plague. But what is remarkable is that God would reward him with a permanent right to the priesthood, not just for him but all his descendants. This should be an excellent example for us today in these tumultuous times that one man's stand for God's righteousness in times of His wrath can make a difference!

We see in chapter twenty-six that after weeding out more Israelites—who were not obedient to God, there would be a second census taken amongst the nation. The first census, taken thirty-eight years earlier, was about the nation's military organization. Now, this one is very significant, for this is to count those who were able and ready to go to battle for the Lord.

Their organizational plans were initially prudent, but now the true test lies in this new generation. Will their zeal, boldness, and trust lie faithfully in the Almighty God who is leading them to the Promise Land? The original generation is gone because of their disobedience. The next generation in this recount is critical because their committed spirit will be essential to their eminent success. Would this be the generation of people that would devote themselves wholeheartedly to God and be His true representatives; after the first generation let Him down?

God's love, patience, and mercy in giving His children another chance is beyond my comprehension! And we'll see God's undeniable divine characteristics come to the surface after His children are blindly counseled to acts of godlessness, which brings forth God's fierce anger. And as we will see in people like Balaam, those who are stumbling blocks can lead others down a path of destruction. But even in our blind choices, God forgives and offers you and me second chances, if not more.

These types of adversaries can be our worst enemies because of their misleading and mischievous ways; they can charm us into the evilest traps of life. And unfortunately, when the Israelites allowed these acts of falsehood to lead to their own stumbling away from God—and their malicious acts against Him, they would be slaughtered!

Any act of being a stumbling block is severe in the eyes of our Lord. After Peter rebuked Jesus, denying the crucifixion would take place, Matt 16:23 tells us, "Jesus turned to Peter and said, "Get away from me, Satan! You are a dangerous trap to me. You are seeing things merely from a human point of view, not from God's."

Jesus even reminds us in Matt 18:5-7, "And anyone who welcomes a little child like this on my behalf is welcoming me. But if you cause one of these little ones who trusts in me to fall into sin, it would be better for you to have a large millstone tied around your neck and be drowned in the depths of the sea. "What sorrow awaits the world because it tempts people to sin. Temptations are inevitable, but what sorrow awaits the person who does the tempting."

It is vitally important, as Christians, that we refrain from being a stumbling block and never lead another into sin. An excellent biblical example of a person who could be classified as a stumbling block is someone who keeps another from a growing and close relationship with God. This topic should never be taken lightly because that one act of being a stumbling block could lead a person down the path of no return.

This is crucial for Christ-followers because we're either a stumbling block—disabling and not enhancing a person's Christlike walk. Or we're a stepping stone—assisting, aiding, and advancing a person's walk with the Lord and enabling them to make things right with God. Acting in this manner portrays our Christlike love, patience, and self-control. And this is pleasing to God because He loves to extend His mercy and unbelievable patience!

Ps 86:15 says it well: "But you, O Lord, are a God merciful and gracious, slow to anger and filled with unfailing love and faithfulness." Micah 7:18 also says, "Where is another God like you, who pardons the guilt of the remnant, overlooking the sins of his special people? You will not stay angry with your people forever because you delight in showing unfailing love."

The Bible contains people who received second and even third and fourth chances: Peter, Jonah, Mark, Samson, David, and others. These people are all trophies of God's grace, so we're in good company! Like I used to tell the inmates in prison, who always wanted that second chance in life. I always conveyed this message, "You will get that opportunity in life, but it will also hinge on your willingness to 'choose change' for the good!"

Even when you feel like you've messed things up the first time, our God's love, mercy, and grace are boundless and immeasurable. When God gives us another chance to fulfill our mission in life for His purpose and plan, we should seize it with zeal and absolute faith in the One Who is guiding our way.

So, we should not waste an opportunity to exalt Him in beautiful ways. That's the time to focus on God's unique calling in our life and put our salvation to work. Paul writes in 2 Cor 6:1, "As God's partners, we beg you not to accept this marvelous gift of God's kindness and then ignore it. God says, "At just the right time, I heard you. On the day of salvation, I helped you." Indeed, the "right time" is now. Today is the day of salvation." God's done so much for you and me; He's forgiven us and made us part of His family for a reason.

Our God is the God of second chances because of His undeniable love and mercy for His children! No matter how rebellious and sinful we've been, He always stands ready to forgive us and welcome us home if we genuinely repent and commit our lives to Jesus Christ.

Don't take your sin lightly; it has cost God far more than we realize. But regardless of our stupid acts, God still loves us. He loves us so much that He sent His only Son into the world to give His life for you and me (John 3:16). Don't let another day go by without Him, but turn to Christ and thank Him for forgiving you and making you His child forever. Then God will say, "This son of mine was dead and is alive again; he was lost and is found" (Luke 15:24).[1]

God does everything possible to draw us to repentance, offering forgiveness and second chances (2 Pet 3:9). But if we continue to reject Him, the

1. Graham, "Does God Give Us Second Chances?"

offer is withdrawn, and, at death, there are no more chances (Heb 9:27). God's grace is our model for today and tomorrow. We, too, can offer second chances to other people around us—until a healthy relationship is no longer possible.[2]

> Eph 1:4–8, "Even before he made the world, God loved us and chose us in Christ to be holy and without fault in his eyes. God decided in advance to adopt us into his own family by bringing us to Himself through Jesus Christ. He wanted to do this, and it gave him great pleasure. So, we praise God for the glorious grace he has poured out on us who belong to his dear Son. He is so rich in kindness and grace that he purchased our freedom with the blood of his Son and forgave our sins. He has showered his kindness on us, along with all wisdom and understanding."

2. "What Does the Bible Say About Second Chances?"

CHAPTER 27

Godly Leader

Num 27:15-19, "Then Moses said to the LORD, "O LORD, you are the God who gives breath to all creatures. Please appoint a new man as leader for the community. Give them someone who will guide them wherever they go and lead them into battle, so the community of the LORD will not be like sheep without a shepherd." The LORD replied, "Take Joshua, son of Nun, who has the Spirit in him and lay your hands on him. Present him to Eleazar, the priest, before the whole community, and publicly commission him to lead the people."

Moses did not complain or argue with God that he would not be the one to lead the children into the Promise Land. This is because he was more concerned about the people. So, Moses asked God to appoint the nation a leader who was externally and internally capable. One who could lead them into battle but also had sincere compassion and care for the people, for that is where a leader gains the trust and respect of a nation. A godly leader is not only focused on completing the plan for God at every command but they are also people-oriented.

Even though Moses had flaws, his genuine care for God's children is seen in his conversation with God. You could sense that Moses did not want to leave His work just to anyone, but he wanted to make sure it was someone ready to fulfill the task for God 100%. What we also see in this powerful passage is that Moses did not recommend a name to God; he asked God for help in selecting the right person for the role. And when God told Moses to take Joshua, Moses worked cooperatively with him to ensure a smooth transition.

This is so important because the work of the Lord requires specific details to its finest point.

We see a beautiful portrait of a selfless, obedient, humble, and modest servant of the Lord when Moses even told the Israelites that Joshua had the ability and complete authority to lead God's children to the Promise Land. And to make the selection process less complicated, it was easy for God to pick Joshua, for he had the Spirit within him.

Joshua, for years, was a faithful and humble servant for Moses and the nation, but most importantly, he was committed to God's purpose and plan! Joshua proved he was a man filled with the power of God's Spirit! After all, the proactive plan for the grooming of Joshua to be a leader of the nation of Israel began soon after they had left Egypt. After passing through their first crisis of no water and no food, when the Lord supplied both miraculously, they were attacked by the Amalekites. Joshua was chosen to recruit an army to fight against them and eventually gained the victory.

And today, as believers, we have the same indwelling Spirit of Christ alive and at work within us, but the key is, are we allowing Him to fill us daily? Does our walk and talk line up with the Fruit of the Spirit? In our lives, we can lead others to Christ, exemplifying Christlikeness to anyone God puts in our path.

Leaders have a high responsibility as shepherds, but as followers of Christ, we also have a high standard to be that shining light and Citizens of Heaven on Earth. To walk in the Spirit is to be filled with the Spirit, illuminating thankfulness, singing, praising, and being joyous (Eph 5:18–20; Col 3:16). Those who walk in the Spirit yearn for the Lord and yield to His calling. They "let the richness of God's word dwell in them deeply" (Col 3:16) while allowing the teaching, rebuking, correcting, and counseling in righteousness to prevail in their life (2 Tim 3:16).

Their entire way of life is lived according to the guides of the gospel as the Spirit moves them toward obedience and truth. When we walk in the Spirit, we find that the sinful appetites of the flesh have no more dominion over us. Our spirit-filled lives become second nature and make it easier to turn away from the evilness that can consume us. But only if we're filled. And guess what? It doesn't cost us anything—because the Holy Spirit is always there—ready to lead the submissive and willing servant to the next phase of their godly purpose and plan for the Lord.

A godly leader, like Moses, and we will see in Joshua, is more concerned about the more significant task at hand for God's glory. They know their strength in fulfilling this role will come from the Lord, not their own power. A God-fearing leader also focuses on each specific detail to God's standards, not man's way. They think of and look at ways to influence others in Christlikeness while exhibiting humility, patience, and passion for their peers and others involved with the mission.

They constantly seek God's direction, and their words of leadership consist of clarity with grace and love. They always portray themselves as peacemakers, in complete unity and kindness, not divisiveness. They know how to resolve conflicts biblically and when and how to implement mercy. Fairness and honorable deeds are garnished within their traits because they listen more than they talk—while learning from their team members as a means of encouragement and motivation. Their discerning spirit leads them to select and surround themselves with people who are trustworthy and committed to the goal 100%!

A godly leader also recognizes the value and qualities of other people. They continually invest their time and effort in them—because it syncs the team as one with the same common goal in mind. A good leader encourages and supports others, for they inspire and foster a positive and Christlike environment. Their gentleness and joy of doing God's work will lead them to be slow to anger because they are consistently spirit-minded. They become the best Christlike follower because they exemplify integrity, self-control, and accountability. Their godly example is evident because they assume complete authority and ownership under God's guidance. They are driven with earnestness to take others where a man cannot take them, only God!

When you read this array of undeniable attributes of a godly leader, we can see that this is so important in our homes, schools, communities, and churches. And to be honest, godly leaders are needed in every facet of a leadership role because without them in the most key and vital positions, there will never be change for the good! So, sit back and let that sink in.

If we want to see scriptural and God-leading alterations in our society and culture today, we need people with these fruitful characteristics to come to the forefront. They are needed now more than ever. Below are a few quotes from well-known people about leadership, but most specifically, a godly leader.

- "If your actions inspire others to dream more, learn more, do more, and become more, you are a leader." —John Quincy Adams

- "The greatest leader is not necessarily the one who does the greatest things. He is the one that gets the people to do the greatest things." —Ronald Reagan

- "A leader knows the way, goes the way, and shows the way." —John C. Maxwell

- "Leadership is not about titles, positions, or flowcharts. It is about one life influencing another." —John C. Maxwell

- "The supreme quality of leadership is integrity." —Dwight D. Eisenhower

- "Outstanding leaders go out of their way to boost the self-esteem of their personnel. If people believe in themselves, it's amazing what they can accomplish." —Sam Walton

- "A genuine leader is not in search of consensus, but a molder of consensus." —Martin Luther King, Jr.

- A spiritual leader will, first and foremost, have a calling from God. His work will not be his profession but his calling. *Zac Poonen*

- The authority by which the Christian leader leads is not power but love, not force but example, not coercion but reasoned persuasion. Leaders have power, but power is safe only in the hands of those who humble themselves to serve. John Stott

- Remember that mentor leadership is all about serving. Jesus said, "For even the Son of Man came not to be served but to serve others and to give his life as a ransom for many" (Mark 10:45). *Tony Dungy*[1]

---

1. Lamoureaux, "Thirty-Seven Christian Leadership Quotes."

CHAPTER 28

Pleasing God

Num 28:1–2, "The LORD said to Moses, "Give these instructions to the people of Israel: The offerings you present as special gifts are a pleasing aroma to me; they are my food. See to it that they are brought at the appointed times and offered according to my instructions."

Offerings presented to God had to be brought regularly, and they had to be presented according to God's prescribed rituals, which the priests supervised. These sacrifices belonged to God, which means His commands could not be improvised one bit. The appointed time is daily; each day began and ended with this statement of the need for atonement by sacrifice—with the expression of devotion to the Lord.

Later in this chapter, it shows that you shall offer in the morning and the evening. This should remind us that it is appropriate to begin and end the day with a statement of trust in God's atonement and expression of our devotion to Him.

It took a lot of work and dedication to be a priest and fulfill God's commanded offerings to His specifications: Every day, every week, every month, and many times a year required special sacrifices. These ceremonies took time, but an important note is that they allowed people to prepare their hearts for worship!

We should be like David when he says in Ps 5:3, "Listen to my voice in the morning, Lord. Each morning I bring my requests to you and wait expectantly." And like the descendants of Korah in Ps 88:13, "O Lord, I cry out to you. I will keep on pleading day by day."

Prepping ourselves in daily devotion first thing in the morning builds a heart and mindset for focusing all our attention on the Lord throughout the day (Col 3:1–2). If we only had the same outright faithfulness as the priests possessed in their commitment to God—in offering sweet aromas to the throne of God with such praise, admiration, honor, and thanksgiving for all He has done and is doing—how much would that bless our Holy Father!

"We often speak of ourselves as hungering or thirsting for God, but do we sufficiently realize that He hungers for our love, wholehearted commitment, and fellowship with Him? If we really love Jesus as King and Lord, we should be eager and yearning to give Him our daily food in prayer, with a yielding faith and obedience in our everyday activities. We should long with an intense desire for Him to be satisfied and pleased with our offerings to Him."[1] Oh, what a sweet fragrance that would be if only our hearts were so devoted to Him in that manner!

The heart must be genuinely changed for a person to be saved and transformed, leading to a life honoring God in all His ways. This only happens through the power of God's Spirit in response to faith in Jesus Christ. In His grace, God can create a new heart within us (Ps 51:10; Ezek 36:26). He promises to "revive the heart of the contrite ones" (Isaiah 57:15).

God's work of creating a new heart within us involves testing our hearts (Ps 17:3; Deut 8:2) and filling them with His desires. But the key is preparing and protecting our hearts from the corrupt ways of the world. This is vital because the heart is the core of our being, and the Bible sets high importance on keeping our hearts pure: "Above all else, guard your heart, for it is the wellspring of life" (Prov 4:23). God knows the secrets of the heart and what steps of preparation we're taking each day (Ps 44:21).

And the key is this; a Christ-centered person "cannot endure living in disharmony with God" and will quickly confess sin and be restored to fellowship with Him. This process of living in continual harmony with God is called sanctification. It is a lifelong process that should show daily progress by which God makes us more like Jesus (Rom 8:29; Heb 12:14). When we "first" center our hearts on Him, our lives as His servants quickly follow. As a Christian, if you need a daily checklist that would show things that are pleasing to our Heavenly Father, it would simply be this:

- Walk by Faith and not by sight. Genuine saving faith pleases God. We cannot do anything pleasing to God "without faith." 2 Cor 5:7, Heb 11:6

- Be Submissive to His Authority. Jas 4:7, 1 Pet 5:6, Prov 3:5–6

1. "Numbers 28—Sacrifices for Appointed Days and Feasts."

- Be Spiritually Minded, exemplifying the Fruit of the Spirit. Rom 8:5–7, Gal 5:22–23

- Don't Grieve the Holy Spirit. 1 Thess 5;19, Eph 4:30–31, Isa 63:10

- Fear God. Prov 1:7, 3;7, 9:10, Ps 111:10, Eccl 12;13

- Be Imitators of Christ; possess a Christlike Attitude of Humility, Service, and Love. 1 Cor 11:1, Eph 5:1–2, 1 John 2:6, 1 Pet 2:21, Phil 3:17

- Obey the Lord. John 14:15, 1 John 5:3, Deut 27:10, 30:10, Jer 7:23

- Do God's Will. 1 Thess, 4:13, 1 Peter 2:15, Mark 3:35, Ps 40:8

- Be Students of His Word. 2 Tim 3:16–17, 2 Tim 2:15, Ps 119:105,

- Be Living Sacrifices. Rom 12:1–2, Col 3:17, 1 Cor 6:19–20

Christ reminds us in John 8:29, "And the one who sent me is with me—he has not deserted me. For I always do what pleases him." This short and powerful message by Jesus Christ clearly shows us in these profound words that the presence of the Father in Him is seen in "every" act and moment of His life—all things done by Him were always in accordance with the Father's will. That is a huge order and a high benchmark for us to follow daily.

But here's encouraging and comforting news: The Bible mentions throughout the New Testament that the Holy Spirit gives us the power to live godly lives pleasing to God. He teaches us and guides us (John 14:26), He comforts us and bears witness of Christ (John 15:26), and He sanctifies us and makes us like Christ (1 Pet 1:2). His availability is always there to help us in our cause of Christ and doing things that pleases God.

And there is no doubt that when we faithfully live by the greatest commandments of all, we're living a life that is honoring and pleasing to Him daily. Matt 22:36–40, "Teacher, which is the most important commandment in the law of Moses?" Jesus replied, "'You must love the LORD your God with all your heart, all your soul, and all your mind.' This is the first and greatest commandment. A second is equally important: 'Love your neighbor as yourself.' The entire law and all the demands of the prophets are based on these two commandments."

CHAPTER 29

Godly Examination

> Num 29:1, "Celebrate the Festival of Trumpets each year on the first day of the appointed month in early autumn. You must call an official day for holy assembly, and you may do no ordinary work."

In this chapter, three festivals were set aside during this season (the seventh month) for the Israelites.

These holidays provided a time to refresh and reset their mind and body and renew their commitment to God. But most noticeably, in the Festival (Feast) of Trumpets, there's an essential emphasis on worship, which was all the people gathering to celebrate, praise, and honor God. Their normal daily routine was to be suspended, and the people "gave God something of value," and it was to be their best.

Later in Jewish tradition, this feast became the time of the new year that we now know as Rosh Hashanah. This holiday marked the beginning of ten days of repentance and consecration before God, culminating on Yom Kippur, or the Day of Atonement. On this final day, Jewish tradition holds that God opens the Book of Life and studies the words, actions, and thoughts of every person whose name is written there.

For Israel to obey God, based on His requirements in Numbers chapters 28–29, they would have to sacrifice almost eleven hundred lambs yearly along with all the bulls, rams, thousands of bottles of oil, wine, and tons of oil. There are estimates that during Jesus' day, over two-hundred fifty thousand lambs were sacrificed at just one Passover. But here's the most compelling point—thousands of these sacrifices were never enough to take away a person's sin. Only One sacrifice would atone for them all!

The Law of Moses required animal sacrifices to atone for all the sins in Israel. As we can see throughout the Old Testament, many sacrifices were made. And sadly, the same sacrifices were repeated endlessly year after year (Heb 10:1). All sin had to be atoned for, including sin committed by an ordinary person (Lev 4:27), the priests (Lev 4:3), the leaders (Lev 4:22), and the nation as a whole (Lev 4:13). In addition to the sacrifices made for sin were offerings for ceremonial cleansing, which involved no moral failing, and voluntary sacrifices made in thanksgiving to God.

If we sit back and ponder on the mere number of animals required to fulfill the requirements of the Mosaic Law, it makes me wonder, "How in the world could the Israelites keep up." The key is that livestock was always near and usually plentiful in the rural culture of their day. It's almost as if God was saying, "I will bless you with enough so that you can offer heartfelt sacrifices of your best—and bless Me in return."

Blessing God is our praises and thanksgiving to Him while exalting and worshipping Him for everything He has done for us. Undoubtedly, God knew that His children would continue to sin, and He would provide them with enough sacrificial offerings, enabling His children to show His mercy and love through their obedience. But this could only be done "properly" from a repentant heart, which glorifies God.

For us as Christians today, do we keep committing the same sin over and over? When is it enough? Will God continue to forgive us for repeated sins? He does remind us, "As far as the east is from the west, so far has He removed our transgressions from us" (Ps 103:12). And in 1 John 1:9, "If we confess our sins, He is faithful and just and will forgive us our sins and purify us from all unrighteousness." What an incredible promise! God will forgive our sins—when we come to Him with genuine repentance. God's grace is so great and immeasurable that it can cleanse the sinner; even when they stumble—He still forgives.

But here's a key point and takeaway for God's children. It is not biblical for a person to sin habitually and be a follower of Christ (1 John 3:8–9). Paul warns us to "Examine yourselves to see whether you are in the faith; test yourselves" (2 Cor 13:5). As Christians, we stumble but do not continue to live a lifestyle of unrepentant sin.

Grace is a gift from God that should not be abused (Eph 2:8). When we sin, the Spirit will convict us in such a powerful way that a godly sorrow will result (2 Cor 7:10–11), and a genuine representative of Christ will act upon that conviction. And by our "real" life, His grace is shown by being sanctified daily!

I love this analogy of the Holy Spirit known as the five C's: 1) He 'convicts' us of our wrongdoings, 2) He 'counsels' the humble and contrite heart.

3) He 'corrects' us and helps us to get back on the path of righteousness, 4) He 'comforts' us through the process, and 5) He communicates the truth to us. We need these five phases to ensure we're headed in the right direction in our daily lives.

One of the most powerful chapters addressing being freed from sin, which lies in the status of our genuine sanctification, is found in Romans chapter six. This section covers and deals with our sanctification stage in our Christian walk. This period in our lives as Christ-followers is the change God makes in us through the power of His Spirit once we accept Jesus Christ as our Savior and Lord. This chapter's preface starts by saying, "Well then, should we keep on sinning so God can show us more and more lovingkindness and forgiveness?" The answer is, "Of course not"!

If we know God's mercy is immeasurable, and forgiveness is His promise and guarantee—can't we continue to use that freedom as believers and continue to sin—so He can bestow upon us His mercy even more? No! That type of attitude, which is almost like premeditating sinful acts ahead, is also taking advantage of God's loving character. Again, we must remember the examples of the Israelites; God's continued forgiveness does not make our sins less severe because, over time, there could be dire consequences for our continuous unholy acts. Christ died once for all our sins, which is a beautiful portrait that we should not return to the foot of the cross, time after time, with the same old sin.

The availability of God's mercy and love must never become a ridiculous excuse and scapegoat for careless and immoral living. The author in Hebrews reminds us in chapter six of this book, "So let us stop going over the basic teachings about Christ repeatedly. Let us go on instead and become mature in our understanding. Surely, we don't need to start again with the fundamental importance of repenting from evil deeds and placing our faith in God." In other words, mature Christians should not only be teaching new Christians the fundamental and core beliefs of God's word but also putting into practice what they know from Scripture in their own life.

Peter even reminds us, powerfully, in his second epistle that we have every resource for living a godly life, which means we don't have any excuses for our habitual foolish acts. Peter also tells us in 2 Peter that when we continue to grow in our faith, work out our salvation, pay attention to the scriptures, and put it into practice, knowledge and experience will give us greater confidence in the message to live it out wholeheartedly. And in our daily examination as Christians, that should be our number one objective.

1 John 3:4–9, "Everyone who sins is breaking God's law, for all sin is contrary to the law of God. And you know that Jesus came to take away our sins, and there is no sin in him. Anyone who continues to live in Him will not

sin. But anyone who keeps on sinning does not know him or understand who he is. Dear children, don't let anyone deceive you about this: When people do what is right, it shows they are righteous, even as Christ is righteous."

"But when people continue sinning, it shows they belong to the devil, who has been sinning since the beginning. But the Son of God came to destroy the works of the devil. Those who have been born into God's family do not make a practice of sinning because God's life is in them. So, they can't keep on sinning because they are children of God."

These impactful passages tell us that the authentic ideal Christian frame of mind and heart realizes the importance of the absence of willful sinning. Yes, they will stumble and often fall, but intentional lawlessness is not their predisposition or prerequisite in life. Christ died at the hands of those who did not know Him. But we know Him, which should incentivize us to know by His wounds that we are healed and aim to live in righteousness. On the other hand, continual sins show that we're still spiritually sick—and a proper spiritual examination will reveal our sickness. God has the antidote: "absolute genuine saving faith" in Jesus Christ.

Heb 10:20–29, "By his death, Jesus opened a new and life-giving way through the curtain into the Most Holy Place. And since we have a great High Priest who rules over God's house, let us go right into the presence of God with sincere hearts, fully trusting him. For our guilty consciences have been sprinkled with Christ's blood to make us clean, and our bodies have been washed with pure water. Let us hold tightly without wavering to the hope we affirm, for God can be trusted to keep his promise. Let us think of ways to motivate one another to acts of love and good works. And let us not neglect our meeting together, as some people do, but encourage one another, especially now that the day of his return is drawing near."

"Dear friends, if we deliberately continue sinning after we have received knowledge of the truth, there is no longer any sac-rifice that will cover these sins. There is only the terrible expec-tation of God's judgment and the raging fire that will consume his enemies. For anyone who refused to obey the law of Moses was put to death without mercy on the testimony of two or three witnesses. Just think how much worse the punishment will be for those who have trampled on the Son of God, and have treated the blood of the covenant, which made us holy, as if it were common and unholy, and have insulted and disdained the Holy Spirit who brings God's mercy to us."

CHAPTER 30

Godly Integrity

Num 30: 1–2, "Then Moses summoned the leaders of the tribes of Israel and told them, "This is what the LORD has commanded: A man who makes a vow to the LORD or makes a pledge under oath must never break it. He must do "exactly what he said he would do.""

Moses gathered the leaders and reminded them of the importance of when they made a vow that it could not be broken. In those days, they did not have written contracts; their commitments were based on their words and were as binding as a signature. But to make the vow more binding, they would give an offering along with the promise. If they broke it, they fractured their trust—then their reputation is tainted, and relationships are shattered.

God includes these guidelines in His word to show us that a vow before God is no small thing. Why? Because a promise from man to others and even God Himself illustrates if we have the same principles and morals as our Heavenly Creator. God expressly commanded that Israel be careful to keep its vows and fulfill every oath they made, and this same command applies to everyone today.

We see in these passages that vows are sacred and should never be considered lightly. So, God enforces strong and clear safeguards against the abuse of this most blessed topic. A great analogy for us to implement in our daily lives about keeping our word is this: God's word and promises are consistent and factual, for God is not a liar. One of His most divine characteristics is based on truth and not wavering, for He's the same yesterday, today, and forever, and that should be our mindset.

A commonly overlooked and unappreciated sin among God's people is the sin of *broken vows*—promising things to God and failing to live up to that commitment. Under the old covenant, it was commanded to make an offering to atone for the breaking of vows (Lev 5:4). Therefore, those who honor God:

- Will not be quick to make vows to God, especially unwise vows.
- Will be serious about fulfilling vows they do make.
- Will regard broken vows as sins to be confessed and to be repented of.

Some people today believe that vows or oaths are not permitted for a Christian today. They think this because of what Jesus said in Matt 5:34–37: " But I say, do not make any vows! Do not say, 'By heaven!' because Heaven is God's throne. And do not say, 'By the earth!' because the Earth is his footstool. And do not say, 'By Jerusalem!' for Jerusalem is the city of the great King. Do not even say, 'By my head!' for you can't turn one hair white or black. Just say a simple, 'Yes, I will,' or 'No, I won't.' Anything beyond this is from the evil one."

But, in the context of the rest of Scripture, we see that Jesus was not forbidding oaths, as much as telling us that we should be so filled with integrity in our words that an oath is unnecessary. Jesus answered under oath in a court (Matt 26:63–64), and God Himself swears oaths (Luke 1:73, Acts 2:30, Heb 3:18, 6:13, 17).

However, and this is important, there is a regular vow we all can and should make daily, and that is a vow of praise, thanksgiving, commitment, and honor to God: "I will fulfill my vows to you, O God, and will offer a sacrifice of thanks for your help" (Ps 56:12). Then I will sing praises to your name forever as I fulfill my vows each day" (Ps 61:8).[1] If we were consistently faithful to our promises to God, it may shed light on our level of being more responsible and accountable Christians.

In the Old Testament, the Hebrew word translated as "integrity" means "the condition of being without blemish, completeness, perfection, sincerity, soundness, uprightness, and wholeness." Integrity in the New Testament means "honesty and adherence to a pattern of good works." And for us, Jesus is our perfect example of a Man of integrity to follow. After He was baptized, He went into the wilderness, fasting for forty days and nights. During that time, Satan came to Him at His weakest to break His integrity and corrupt Him. But in all the enemy's all-out attempts, he could not break the integrity of Christ! And today, Christians are called to be the examples of Jesus Christ—He's our daily benchmark!'

---

1. "Numbers 30—The Keeping of Vows."

Today, breaking an oath is just standard business practice—*but before God*, it is simply a sin because it fractures our character in Christlike integrity. Anything that separates us from God's word and truth will isolate us from His purpose and plan. Most importantly, (as stated earlier) an attribute of God's nature is His trustworthiness, so any act we commit that does not align with His characteristics is a sin.

Our trust is broken when we give our word but fail to follow through with those affected. Even today, our words are our bond! And when we break our promise or word with a brother or sister in Christ or anyone, we have just fractured that unity with God. How can we be respectable and reliable representatives of Jesus Christ if we have a reputation of—"Stay away from them because they are untrusting?" We do more damage to our testimony if we have a tainted reputation.

Integrity is the quality of honesty and strong moral principles, and uprightness. It's the state of being whole and undivided. In other words, when we're abiding by God's character, "the lack of integrity" is not part of our makeup—because we're enwrapped with righteous and holy living.

One with Christlike integrity upholds unity and wholeness in His attributes. They are sound in their loyalty to the Lord, stable and unwavering, knowing that their identity lies in His integrity. Their promise and commitment are like a rock because their words are solidified with security; it's a given! Can you even fathom if there was a law today that held every individual accountable for their committed words or deeds?

"Integrity" implies moral honesty, honorable, right-minded, and respectable godly standards. Christians should be those who cannot be bribed or compromised to the corruptible ways of the world because we serve God rather than men (Col 3:17, 23; Acts 5:29). We are to be His righteous people who keep our word, no matter what (Matt 5:37; Jas 5:12).

When we are known as Christians with integrity and prone to keep our word, we are less likely to even tell "a little white lie"—because we adhere to the truth no matter what. Keeping our promises to others shows that our love in word and deed is Christlike and illustrates Whose path we're following. (1 John 3:17–18; Jas 2:17–18; Eph 4:29). Living with integrity in a society and culture where the corrupt always seem favored is undoubtedly challenging.

But 1 Pet 3:13–16 encourages us in the word, "Now, who will want to harm you if you are eager to do good? But even if you suffer for doing what is right, God will reward you for it. So don't worry or be afraid of their threats. Instead, you must worship Christ as the Lord of your life. And if someone asks about your hope as a believer, always be ready to explain it. But do this in a gentle and respectful way. Keep your conscience clear. Then if people speak against you, they will be ashamed when they see what a good life you live because you belong to Christ."

In this life on earth, it will be humanly impossible to prevent people from shooting those fiery arrows of spewing evil words against us. But if our Christlike integrity is intact by all the grace, mercy, and love He abounds, it can minimize their ammunition. If we do right in God's eyes and meet His expectations, nothing else should matter, for it is better to suffer for doing good than evil.

> Prov 10:9, "People with integrity walk safely, but those who follow crooked paths will be exposed.

> Prov 11:3, "Honesty guides good people; dishonesty destroys treacherous people."

> Prov 20:7, "The godly walk with integrity; blessed are their children who follow them."

> Philippians 4:8–9, "And now, dear brothers and sisters, one final thing. Fix your thoughts on what is true, and honorable, and right, and pure, and lovely, and admirable. Think about things that are excellent and worthy of praise. Keep putting into practice all you learned and received from me—everything you heard from me and saw me doing. Then the God of peace will be with you."

CHAPTER 31

God's Instructions

Num 31:1–7, "Then the LORD said to Moses, "On behalf of the people of Israel, take revenge on the Midianites for leading them into idolatry. After that, you will die and join your ancestors." So, Moses said to the people, "Choose some men, and arm them to fight the LORD's war of revenge against Midian. From each tribe of Israel, send 1,000 men into battle." So, they chose 1,000 men from each tribe of Israel, a total of 12,000 men armed for battle. Then Moses sent them out, 1,000 men from each tribe, and Phinehas, son of Eleazar, the priest, led them into battle. They carried along the holy objects of the sanctuary and the trumpets for sounding the charge. They attacked Midian as the LORD had commanded Moses, and they killed all the men."

A significant emphasis in this passage is that the LORD spoke to Moses in initiating this attack—it wasn't about personal revenge, the conquest of territory, or the lust for plunder. "The war is announced by the Lord, not Moses." And Moses did not regard the war as motivated by petty jealousy. It was 'the Lord's vengeance' because of the wickedness of the Midianites, who caused the seduction of the Israelites in the pagan worship system of Baal of Peor." Because the LORD specifically declared this war, this was also a test of Israel's obedience to Him and not taking matters into their own hands.[1]

God will not allow evilness amongst His children, and when others try to lead them away from the will of His plan, there will be a price to pay. For example, God commanded that the Midianites be attacked in retribution for their seduction of Israel into sexual immorality and idolatry. Here, the

---

1. "Numbers 31—Vengeance on Midian."

Midianites who were associated with Moab are picked out for vengeance. Always remember that vengeance belongs to God, and when it comes to misleading His people, it's personal and in God's hands. Disobedience was so rampant in the past that a Psalmist even cried out, "Rivers of tears gushed from his eyes because people disobey Your instructions" (Ps 119:136). Undoubtedly, disobedience is still rampant today, and many want to take matters into their own hands.

As Christians, we should be uncomfortable with the fleshly idea of vengeance because it doesn't seem consistent with God's love, mercy, and grace. Yet, in its right circumstance, vengeance is something good where God will act. In the scriptures, we must remember that the nation of Israel "received a special call to be an instrument of God's vengeance, not man."

A personal note: Revenge is something we should never take upon ourselves. Israel had this unique role as part of God's plan. God's vengeance is to punish those who have offended and rejected Him—especially when their motives do not align with His purpose and plan. Unfortunately, when humans want to take vengeance upon their own, in so many cases, they are more controlled by the flesh and not by the Spirit. We can, however, pray for God to avenge Himself in perfection and holiness against His enemies and to avenge those who are oppressed by evil.

It is tempting for all of us to try and take on the role of God and seek to punish those who "we feel" may deserve it. But because we are of a sinful nature, it is impossible for us to take revenge with pure and righteous motives. Christians must follow the Lord Jesus' command to "Love your enemies and pray for those who persecute you," leaving the vengeance to God (Matt 5:44).

In Deuteronomy, God speaks of the stubborn, rebellious, idolatrous Israelites who rejected Him and incurred His wrath "with their wickedness." He promised to avenge Himself upon them in His timing and according to His perfect and pure motives. Unlike us, *God never takes vengeance from impure motives.*

Biblically speaking, if we conducted an in-depth research on why many people take vengeance into their own hands, we would discover that it's selfish, leading to unrighteous and sinful acts. Why? Because it leads to devastating results (nothing positive comes from it), and it's corruptible. Deliberate and calculated revenge is self-defeating and foolish, and in the end, it's fruitless, and our efforts would be futile—because God was never part of the equation.

Paul reminds us in Galatians chapter five that only two forces are at work and cannot co-exist—we're either controlled by the flesh or the Spirit. These most precious nine elements of the Fruit of the Spirit should be our measuring stick for godly instructions in our daily lives. They are love, joy, peace, patience, kindness, goodness, faithfulness, gentleness, and self-control. If we look at the order of these essential Christlike attributes, we will see that if the first fruit, love, consumes our Christian life consistently, these other beautiful features will lead us to be more in control of all matters in life.

If we don't relinquish all our dire circumstances into God's Almighty hands, we will never be at peace with forgiveness. Our consuming flesh will want to continue with more and more anger and resentment, which opens the gateway to more sin in our life. And this is not spiritually healthy and will never be pleasing to God.

One of the most significant indicators that we're following God's instructions is when we let go of self, obey Him through all the "thick and thin," know that our utmost faith is resting in Him, exemplifying Christlikeness no matter what—and let God be God! God has linked love, faith, and obedience together so that all the promises of God are conditioned upon you and me, following every direction He gives us in His word.

"Man must evolve for all human conflict, a method which rejects revenge, aggression, and retaliation. The foundation of such a method is love." — Martin Luther King, Jr.

"The alternate domination of one faction over another, sharpened by the spirit of revenge natural to party dissension, which in different ages and countries 'has perpetrated the most horrid enormities,' is a frightful despotism." — George Washington.

God's word reminds us in Lev 19:18, "'Do not seek revenge or bear a grudge against anyone among your people but love your neighbor as yourself. I am the Lord.'" God consistently tells us throughout His word that all His rules are rooted in what Jesus said, Love the Lord your God with all your heart, soul, and mind, and your neighbor as yourself.

In other words, if we carry out this simple command by our Savior, as Christians, we will discover that following all His further instructions will become like second nature. And when we get off course, we will know and feel it because we're more yielding to the Holy Spirit and His word.

> Deut 5:32–33, "So be careful to do what the Lord your God has commanded you; do not turn aside to the right or the left. Walk in obedience to all that the Lord your God has commanded you, so that you may live and prosper and prolong your days in the land you will possess."

CHAPTER 32

Going Deep

Num 32:6–12, "Do you intend to stay here while your brothers go across and do all the fighting?" Moses asked the men of Gad and Reuben. "Why do you want to discourage the rest of the people of Israel from going across to the land the LORD has given them? Your ancestors did the same thing when I sent them from Kadesh-barnea to explore the land. After they went up to the valley of Eshcol and explored the land, they discouraged the people of Israel from entering the land the LORD was giving them. Then the LORD was very angry with them, and he vowed... 'Of all those I rescued from Egypt, no one who is twenty years old or older will ever see the land I swore to give to Abraham, Isaac, and Jacob, for they have not obeyed me wholeheartedly. The only exceptions are Caleb, son of Jephunneh the Kenizzite, and Joshua, son of Nun, for they have wholeheartedly followed the LORD.'

Moses feared that the attitude of the tribes of Reuben and Gad would keep the other tribes from entering the Promise Land; he was afraid that their mindset was the same as the previous generation, which was of unbelief. He feared they started to possess an attitude such as, "We've fought enough and suffered enough already. Let's settle down where we're at, we're good, and we're done. We finally accomplished our task, and our job is now finished."

However, Moses wanted them to know that it was not over; they were not done, there was a battle to fight, and they were all in this plan together. Just because these tribes were suddenly content with their current position did not mean their responsibility was over. The generation that died in the wilderness didn't have the faith to enter the Promise Land enthusiastically, obediently, boldly, and confidently. They would rather stay where they were and not move with God, and Moses worried that this same type of unbelief was present among the tribes of Reuben and Gad.

Even for us today, if we're not careful, this could be a danger zone when we keep company with those who are satisfied with what they have in life and have no desire to go into a deeper relationship with God—or press on further biblically and spiritually. Why? Because their fleshly contentment can so often influence us—as is the case in this storyline.

Moses was concerned that if these tribes became complacent, it could dangerously influence the other tribes. But the operative word at the end of this passage is when God tells us, "The only exceptions are Caleb, son of Jephunneh the Kenizzite, and Joshua, son of Nun, for they have wholeheartedly followed the LORD."

As wholehearted Christians and faithful followers of Jesus Christ, does our work ever stop? Aren't we supposed to be His light daily in this dark and gloomy world? Are we supposed to be armed, equipped, and ready to defend our faith and battle against the enemy? Placing our complete confidence in God is what trusting God is all about. When we say "fully or whole," it means full inclusion of everything we are and anything we have—it is wholeheartedly. Wholehearted means a "hundred percent" of confidence placed in God's hands—undivided—and nothing is left behind. [1]

Paul reminds us in Phil 1:6, "And I am certain that God, who began the good work within you, will continue his work until it is finally finished on the day when Christ Jesus returns." We have a lot of work to do as His Citizens of Heaven on Earth in accomplishing this tall task. So, we must go deeper into the richness and fullness of His word to establish that solid bonded relationship and ascertain His wisdom, insight, purpose, and plan with the help of His Spirit!

You probably heard me share this testimony in one of my past books when I was a Chaplain and Mentor at a prison facility. One afternoon in a one-on-one session, this one inmate who started to faithfully attend our services on Wednesday nights, reading God's word, praying without ceasing, and bonding with the brotherhood in Christ suddenly one day said, "He's had enough"! I asked him, "What did he mean by this?" He told me that ever since he started to come to Wednesday night services, pray, read God's word, and associate with the community of believers, the enemy has intensified his weapons, and the spiritual warfare was more than he could bear—he was ready to throw in the towel.

I looked at him in this decisive one-on-one meeting, and the words that would precede from my lips spontaneously were not of me but the work of the

---

1. "Numbers 32—The Tribes Settling East of Jordan."

Holy Spirit. I asked him, "Where in God's word does it say that the enemies will love believers in Jesus Christ, and we won't feel or go through persecution?" "Where does it say our lives will always be peaceful and joyful?" Don't you know that the Lord is glorified as He gives us more and more of His peace and joy, and we enforce it in our life?" "As a Christian, do you think the enemy will leave you alone?" "He will only flee when he knows that a Christian is faithfully committed to the Lord—and there is no wiggle room for him to squeeze into our life with those little temptations."

Don't you remember what we discussed in the powerful book of James? Where it says in Jas 1:2–8, "Dear brothers and sisters when troubles of any kind come your way, consider it an opportunity for great joy. For you know that when your faith is tested, your endurance has a chance to grow. So let it grow, for when your endurance is fully developed, you will be perfect and complete, needing nothing. If you need wisdom, ask our generous God, and he will give it to you. He will not rebuke you for asking. But when you ask him, be sure that your faith is in God alone."

"Do not waver, for a person with divided loyalty is as unsettled as a wave of the sea that is blown and tossed by the wind. Such people should not expect to receive anything from the Lord. Their loyalty is divided between God and the world, and they are unstable in everything they do. So, humble yourselves before God. Resist the devil, and he will flee from you. Come close to God, and God will come close to you. Wash your hands, you sinners; purify your hearts, for your loyalty is divided between God and the world. Let there be tears for what you have done. Let there be sorrow and deep grief. Let there be sadness instead of laughter, and gloom instead of joy. Humble yourselves before the Lord, and he will lift you up in honor."

And don't you remember what James said compellingly in Jas 4:7–8, "So humble yourselves before God. Resist the devil, and he will flee from you. Come close to God, and God will come close to you. Wash your hands, you sinners; purify your hearts, for your loyalty is divided between God and the world."

I looked at him and said, 'It sounds like you want full-time benefits but only want to offer part-time services! I told him, "It sounds like you're still divided on who you are committed to in life and leaving an open space for the enemy." I told him that servanthood does not work this way.' He knew the brotherhood of believers' banner in this facility, "You're either all in or not in at all." But he allowed the enemy to focus more on his weaknesses and past life, not what Christ's strength could do through Him as a new creation.

Here's the synopsis; he did not want to pay the spiritual price of commitment, faithfulness, obedience, patience, endurance, and perseverance—he wanted the sweet life of perfection handed to him on a silver platter. He did not want to offer his life as a living sacrifice wholeheartedly to the Lord. It was more about his comfort zone and not stretching out toward the Zone of Christ—because that takes an earnest spirit willing to work at God's finest point.

We are all flawed and will always be imperfect on this side of Heaven, but when we yield to His Spirit, He will help us to become more like Christ, our Redeemer, even with all those flaws. And when we allow Him to show His power of grace at work in us, it will lift our spirits and strengthen us to not throw in the towel—but strive for that finest stage in our life for His glory.

When Christ used a towel, it was used as a lowly servant honoring His Father (wiping His disciples' feet). It was not used and thrown in as a means of defeat. The Lord was showing us the life of a faithful servant and a more significant cause and case for Christ in spreading His Gospel everywhere! The job for you and me will never be done.

Instead, the enemy attacks us when we attempt to go deeper for our Lord because he wants us to stay right where we are, and not progress in our Christian walk. When we remain right where we are and not moving forward with our Lord, the enemy stands beside us, patting us on the back and making us feel comfortable in that complacency. He's got us right where he wants us, and we fall into the danger zone—because a complacent spirit has lost interest, concern, and all enthusiasm in serving the One who needs us more today than ever.

"A person who wants and desires that more profound and deeper relationship with God possesses a genuine passionate pursuit—wanting more of Him daily." That's their persistent Christlike path because they are now a new creation, died to self, caring for more of His glory in their lives. Their focus has shifted from them to Him and others. They are utterly dissatisfied with their worldly ways and yearn for more of a sincere relationship with their Lord in this long sustainable run of life.

They are eager to understand His wisdom, grace, love, and goodness more. They are in an all-out chase after His most divine nature of holiness. They aim to strive for His righteousness while grasping His forgiveness and justice. They want to be grounded in the truth of His word and Spirit, not the clanging sounds of the world and the enemy! They know there will be obstacles, but their undeniable intent will endure and persevere through turbulent times.

If we want to stay connected with God daily through the power of His Spirit and dive into a deeper relationship with Him, we must press on with the ways of the Lord into our daily lives and allow Him to provide and produce great things in and through us. Going deeper means growing closer and walk-ing with Him side-by-side. It means you are sold out to Jesus no matter the circumstances in life. What does this mean? It illustrates a follower who's; 1) Died to self, 2) Abiding in Him and Him in you, 3) Committed to understand-ing His word and applying it to every area of your life, 4) Possesses a diligent prayer life, 5) Fostering faith-based Christian relationships in your daily life. 6) Obediently and faithfully serving in some capacity, 7) Displaying a contrite heart, 8) Exhibiting a spirit of humility, 9) Consuming a life of worship and praise, and 10) Portraying a transformed life of Christlikeness while not con-forming to the ways of the world.

If these deep-rooted attributes are not present in your daily life, that lack of desire preventing you from going into a deeper relationship with the Lord could be due to the presence of discouraging people around you. These types of people are content right where they are and don't want to press on for more of the Lord. Complacency can be contagious, contaminating, cancerous, and careless, creating spiritual conflict. These are harsh words, but even though "idle hands are the devil's workshop" is not verbatim in the Bible, it has its roots in Scripture. The Lord knew that He needed to be about His Father's business (Luke 2:49), and so should we! Every day!

> Rom 11:33–36, "Oh, how great are God's riches and wisdom and knowledge! How impossible it is for us to understand his decisions and his ways! For who can know the LORD's thoughts? Who knows enough to give him advice? And who has given him so much that he needs to pay it back? For everything comes from him and ex-ists by his power and is intended for his glory. All glory to him forever!" Amen.

CHAPTER 33

Godly Inspiration

Num 33:1–2, "This is the route the Israelites followed as they marched out of Egypt under the leadership of Moses and Aaron. At the LORD's direction, Moses kept a written record of their progress. These are the stages of their march, identified by the different places where they stopped along the way."

In this chapter lies the remarkable record of the journey of Israel from Egypt to the entrance of the Promise Land. As the Israelites prepared to cross the Jordan and conquer Canaan, this second generation needed to remember the faithfulness and goodness of God over the last forty years. Why was this important? Because, just like then and even for us today, remembering God's faithfulness and goodness would prepare them for future challenges. Since we all tend to forget God's past goodness, we should try to create ways to remember that His words and promises will always stand true.

Moses kept records of their journey, geographically but also spiritually! In this journey, they have seen and experienced the Almighty God at work through His promises, provisions, and preparation of His children. God was Omniscient, Omnipresent, and Omnipotent (as always) through their test of times—no matter the temptations or tribulations they would incur. He was always there, displaying His great work right before their eyes for a purpose.

The plagues the Lord brought upon Egypt were not randomly chosen. They intended to humble the people and rebuke their belief in the Egyptian gods because this was all they knew—until God showed up powerfully and gloriously. And even though it took time, this gave them the boldness to leave as conquerors, not as escaping slaves—but freed from the bondage of evilness!

I used to tell inmates in the Prison Ministry that our daily walk with the Lord is a process, but that process should always *lead to progress*—because "progressive" Christlike steps impact lives in so many ways. We should be tracing our spiritual growth not only in a journal, diary, or physical notes but, most importantly, displaying that spirituality for the glory of the Lord so it can inspire others in what He's doing in our lives.

Like then, God knows His children can easily forget all He's done. So, in His love, He always shows us every stage of our life's journey. Through that progress of our sanctified life, He reminds us of what He did, when He did it, where He did it, why He did it, and how He did it. It will not only reinvigorate our spiritual walk to great heights but also so we can share these powerful and beautiful experiences with others as a means of inspiration—and to pass them on. These stages of growth in our Christian walk are like God reminding us of those victories at each progressive step in our life journey!

Our spiritual lives develop and grow through those quality and quiet moments each day with our Creator. They are ever-increasing times of fellowship with our Heavenly Father, Jesus Christ, and the Holy Spirit (1 John chapter five). Spending time in prayer, reading His Word, and meditating on His truths are all part of nurturing our relationship with Him. The more we know Him, the more we become like Him (2 Cor 3:18).

We should look at true spirituality from this perspective—it's not something to be achieved or conquered—it is a progressive journey throughout our Christian life (one spiritual step at a time). Will we have setbacks? Absolutely! But will we have those little victories to share with others that will lift us up, specifically others? Yes! When others see that progression in us, they will see the Lord's intimate, inspirational, inviting, and loving ways in and through us!

We are true inspirations for our Lord when the world sees His faith actively in our daily lives. When the difficult stages occur in a Christians' life, the world should see a response that reflects all the grace, mercy, and love He abounds that can influence others. When our lives of servanthood are illustrated by exemplifying the Fruit of the Spirit, those moments of service have powerful effects on people "at just the right time." When society sees an attitude of gratitude constantly displayed in a Christian, it impacts people's lives in mighty ways. It could be life-changing for one person, but that one matters in God's eyes.

When the community sees more acts of selflessness versus selfishness, it can establish more humility than you can fathom. And when this world sees the peace of Christ rule in our lives during these tumultuous times, it will have a lingering effect. We can inspire others for God's glory when we're abundantly full of Him—it cannot be a portion; it must be all of Him at work in our lives.

When we engage with Him 100%, that engagement can be infectious to so many within our proximity in powerful ways for God's glory.

- "What you are is God's gift to you; what you become is your gift to God."—*Hans urs von Balthasar.*

- "Let God's promises shine on your problems." – Corrie ten Boom

- "If God is your partner, make your plans BIG!" – D.L. Moody

- "You are the only Bible some unbelievers will ever read." – John MacArthur

- "He who lays up treasures on Earth spends his life backing away from his treasures. To him, death is loss. He who lays up treasures in Heaven looks forward to eternity; he's moving daily toward his treasures. To him, death is gain." – Randy Alcorn [1]

George Liele demonstrated a strength of compassion. Born into slavery, Liele was taught to read and write by his slave owners. He attended church but believed God could only love him if he did good things. But he submitted his life to God. His story will challenge those who have grown up in the church or in cultural Christianity to consider the gospel again.

Liele had a talent for teaching and was ordained as the first black pastor in the Baptist church in America. He preached to both white and black members of his church. He was freed by his master in 1776 and later moved his family to Jamaica and started preaching the gospel there. He was thrown in jail while there for preaching the gospel to slaves, but he was released and went right on preaching. He was the first known Baptist missionary, taking the gospel to Jamaica ten years before William Carey went to India. He "left a legacy of slaves and former slaves who knew freedom and rest in Jesus Christ because of his faithful teaching." [2]

> Isaiah 40:31, "But those who trust in the LORD will find new strength. They will soar high on wings like eagles. They will run and not grow weary. They will walk and not faint."

God's power is at work in us when we rise above the difficult stages of life to heights that glorify Him. And it's during these times that we can impact and inspire people's lives all around us. A child of God who continuously tastes His goodness recognizes His blessings, and it's evident through their constant praise and thanksgiving. Incorporating this type of heart will lift others up in

---

1. "Fifty Christian Quotes to Inspire Your Faith Every Day."
2. "Inspiring Stories of God's Power in the Lives of Ordinary Men."

fruitful ways. Godly inspiration starts with you and me showing others "All the Great Things He Has Done in our lives."

CHAPTER 34

God's Boundaries

Num 34:1–5, "Then the LORD said to Moses, "Give these instructions to the Israelites: When you come into the land of Canaan, which I am giving you as your special possession, these will be the boundaries. The southern portion of your country will extend from the wilderness of Zin along the edge of Edom. The southern boundary will begin on the east at the Dead Sea. It will then run south past Scorpion Pass in the direction of Zin. Its southernmost point will be Kadesh–barnea, from which it will go to Hazar–addar, and on to Azmon. From Azmon the boundary will turn toward the Brook of Egypt and end at the Mediterranean Sea."

According to Genesis 15:18 and Joshua 1:4, the land God gave to Israel included everything from the Nile River in Egypt to Lebanon (south to north) and everything from the Mediterranean Sea to the Euphrates River (west to east). On today's map, the land God has stated that belongs to Israel includes everything in modern-day Israel, plus all the territory occupied by the Palestinians (the West Bank and Gaza), and also all or part of the countries Jordan, Lebanon, Egypt, Syria, Saudi Arabia and Iraq. Thus, Israel currently possesses only a fraction of the land God has promised. But He has given His word that the nation of Israel will never cease as long as the sun still shines by day and the moon and stars shine by night (Jer 31:35–37).[1]

The boundaries described in these passages are more significant than the actual land occupied by the Hebrews when Israel entered the Promise Land. And hundreds of years later, under King Solomon, they occupied a more significant part, but still not all the territory God promised. *Israel was*

1. "What is the Land God Promised to Israel?"

required to obey the Law of Moses, and when they failed, God pushed them out of the land. However, God's promise that they will inherit the land still stands. What a beautiful depiction of God's goodness and generosity. He can give us so much more than we can ever fathom.

More than ever, we need to think about our heavenly-bound home—because His promises and provisions will always stand true, even through the test of times! But most notably and essential in this message is that we see God will not continue to allow disobedience. If we're not in line with His will and plan, He will allow us to fall to the sinful desires that are more appeasing to us—more so than His spiritual realm. Paul reminds us in Colossians chapter three to "Fix our thoughts on the realities of Heaven, and not the things of this earth."

A powerful set of scriptures are found in Lev chapter 26:14–39, where God lays out His punishment for disobedience. His message in these passages shows us that He will not tolerate disobedience, and if it continues, He says I will, "Scatter you among the nations and bring out my sword against you. Your land will become desolate, and your cities will lie in ruins. Then, at last, the land will enjoy its neglected Sabbath years as it lies desolate while you are in exile in the land of your enemies. Then the land will finally rest and enjoy the Sabbaths it missed."

They had a set of boundaries of richness and fullness that they could enjoy for generations. Still, they chose to be defiant, which led Almighty God to push them away from His boundary of promises and provisions. Look at the profound message in what God said above; He was so displeased with them that He not only said He would scatter them, but He said this, "Then, at last, the land will enjoy its neglected Sabbath and the land will finally rest and enjoy the Sabbath it missed," because of their rebelling ways against God!

They ignored and neglected the one true day of worshipping and praising our Holy God, the Sabbath. It could not be enjoyed due to their absolute defiance and would only be at rest when they were no longer in the land. Wow! It's like God saying, "I am better off without you in my presence so my day of holiness can truly be honored!" I don't know about you, but that is heart-piercing. God gave His children a choice over the years; they could have experienced peace and prosperity in the land God provided if they would simply obey. But they could not do that, which led to disastrous curses.

When we disobey God, we are dishonoring His Holy name, His word, and teachings because we're not conducting ourselves in the manner He desires and knows is for our well-being. Anything apart from His holy, righteous, sovereign, and good word separates us from His boundaries of holiness. Then that puts us in the position of being disciplined by a Loving and Just God. If we continue to rebel against Him, it will not only bring His punishment but hinder and prevent us from enjoying the riches of God's blessings.

God will not force you and me to obey Him, but if we choose to disobey, we can never experience the peace, joy, and comfort we can have when we rest in His trusting grace. The Israelites' continuous rebellion is an example for us to apply and live by each day. He forced them out of the land He promised because of their constant defiance of His ways. And today, if we continue to disobey God repeatedly, it can lead to a state of reprobate minds—an ungodly position that is dangerous.

Selfishness (pride) is the primary reason for disobedience to God. In today's society and culture, it's apparent that people want to tailor religion to fit their own habits and lifestyles. They want to be called Christians but don't want to change their lives. Why? Because they don't want to answer to any-one except themselves—they are so consumed and wrapped up in their own little world. They've established their fleshly boundary, and it makes them feel good. And unfortunately, they don't want to be held accountable to anyone in life because they enjoy it that much.

However, Jesus said in Matt 7:21–24: "Not everyone who calls out to me, 'Lord! Lord!' will enter the Kingdom of Heaven. Only those who actually do the will of my Father in Heaven will enter. On judgment day, many will say to me, 'Lord! Lord! We prophesied in your name and cast out demons in your name and performed many miracles in your name.' But I will reply, 'I never knew you. Get away from me, you who break God's laws.' "Anyone who listens to my teaching and follows it is wise, like a person who builds a house on solid rock."

When we attempt to customize our lives the way we desire, that type of religion is inaccurate and does not possess a genuine relationship with God through Jesus Christ. However, God's provision extends to you and me today because He desires an ongoing relationship with all of us, especially those de-pendent on Him (Ps 104:21).

Unfortunately, many depend more on other things than the boundar-ies of the spiritual realm, for their eyes and hearts are focused on prosperity/materialism by looking for more money or possessions. Still, as believers, we should look closer at what God desires to provide for us. He intends to help us develop Christlikeness so that we become His salt and light in the world (Matt 5:13–14).

God does not want us to see Him as a source of material possessions—because acquiring earthly things is not the fundamental goal of this Christlike life (Luke 12:15); it's in the realities of Heaven, which is our godly boundary! His boundary stems from an understanding of who we are in Christ because we are created in the image of God with the intent of glorifying Him in all that we say and do. We should refuse to be defined as anything less when we ingrain this into our hearts, soul, and mind.

Biblically speaking, boundaries are related to self-control, which is a Fruit of the Spirit. The Bible commands us to control *ourselves*, whereas our human nature desires to control us (Titus 2:12). This is illustrated in Galatians chapter five when we see the battle of flesh and spirit. If left unchecked with no spiritual examination (2 Cor 13:5), our natural desires can force us into the unspiritual realm and separate us from the boundaries of God.

But a Christian putting God's word into practice with clear, spiritual, and healthy boundaries communicates to others "what is and is not permissible. They will adamantly say, "This is my godly dominion, and no unholy one has the right to interfere." A believer who sees their need for self-control and who wants to take full responsibility for their actions will seek the Lord's help for growth in this character trait. This is vital because establishing our spiritual boundaries is a fruit of submitting to God's will, where He will enable us to make godly choices.[2]

God tells us to humbly control ourselves, lovingly confront sin, graciously accept others, and overcome evil with good (Rom 12:21). Plus, He promises wisdom in every circumstance (James 1:5). We must have discerning spirits so that we can establish godly boundaries in our daily life—because the health of our souls and spirit is at stake in this crazy life today.

Always remember, God differentiates between our needs and wants because "He knows where our treasure is, for our heart is there also" (Matt 6:21). He wants us to know that this world is not our home and what we need more than ever is to shift our focus toward the eternal life awaiting, but still living and serving as His Citizens of Heaven on Earth. The boundaries that He's established for you and me as believers and followers of Christ are immeasurable—more than we could ever fathom, for it is a glory beyond our finite minds! What a reward that awaits His steadfast believers!

> Acts 17:26–28, "From one man he created all the nations throughout the whole earth. He decided beforehand when they should rise and fall and determined their boundaries. "His purpose was for the nations to seek after God and perhaps feel their way toward him and find him—though he is not far from any one of us. For in him we live and move and exist..."

2. "What Are Boundaries and Are They Biblical?"

CHAPTER 35

Godly Influence

Num 35:1-3, "While Israel was camped beside the Jordan on the plains of Moab across from Jericho, the Lord said to Moses, "Command the people of Israel to give to the Levites from their property certain towns to live in, along with the surrounding pasturelands. These towns will be for the Levites to live in, and the surrounding lands will provide pasture for their cattle, flocks, and other livestock."

The tribe of Levi had no possession of their own within the nation of Israel because their inheritance was from the Lord alone (Num 18:20)." *Then the Lord said to Aaron: You shall have no inheritance in their land, nor shall you have any portion among them; I am your portion and your inheritance among the children of Israel."*

However, the Levites had to live somewhere—so God commanded that each tribe give cities to the Levites so they would be spread or scattered throughout the entire nation. The Levites were God's ministers and were to be supported by the tithes and offerings of the people of Israel. They would supply them with homes, livestock, and land needed to sustain themselves in life and serve God in their assigned positions.

In these passages, we see God's desire to distribute the Levites evenly. They were the most spiritually focused Israelites throughout God's chosen people, and He wanted their godly influence distributed throughout the nation. God intended that these ministers go out amongst the people to lead and direct them for the Lord and make an impact on the Kingdom of God! They would care for the people as His devout representatives. Their cause for Yahweh was a huge responsibility, a high calling with lots of authority.

Each tribe was responsible for accommodating these religious teachers as needed. This was vital so they could perform their tasks and preach the word of God, showing His children the importance of prayer and continuous praise to Almighty God. It was a huge benefit for these Levites to dwell among each tribe so they could teach them the knowledge of the Lord and not leave them in darkness and prey to the ways of the enemy. It was considered a privilege for the tribes to give to the Levites, who ministered to them the ways of God and how to be of service and a spiritual influence in their own lives.

But the key lay in this; once they heard the teachings of God, what level of obedience would be incorporated into their daily life? God is supplying the Israelites with His ministers/servants to help encourage them, assure them, and motivate them to follow His teachings—because the Levites had a role in guarding the worship and praise of Yahweh throughout the nation of Israel. Their position of biblical principles was critical for God's children to live by because God desired them to apply His holy guidelines to their lives, keeping them on His path of promises.

And in the same way for us today, as His Christlike and Spirit-filled followers, God expects us to support our pastors/leaders through the necessary means to sustain them—so they can perform their tasks for the Lord and His Kingdom. We need to pray for our pastors and work alongside them so they will possess the boldness, courage, and spiritual wisdom to lead the church in unity. We need to bolster them to effectively work with the leaders and the body of Christ in teaching the truth with confidence and zeal.

And this statement is so important—"As a body, we need to be cognizant of how the enemy can create dissension and division." The body of Christ needs discerning and maturing spirits, not one constantly complaining, moaning, and groaning (like the Israelites) and giving our pastors a hard time. Because this only leads to them carrying a heavy weight of unneeded burdens. When we act selfishly, as if the church is all about us and not the body, we can become a hindrance and a stumbling block to the Gospel.

Believers must understand that our pastors are God's representatives and church leaders. We all should attend with an ear, mind, and heart to his teaching—value him highly for his work, trust his judgment, wisdom, and experience, and pray for him and his family. But most importantly, pray that the Truth is taught biblically in ways that will rock the foundations of Heaven.

God's word reminds us in Hebrews 13:17 says, "Obey your spiritual leaders, and do what they say. Their work is to watch over your souls, and they are accountable to God. Give them reason to do this with joy and not with sorrow. That would certainly not be for your benefit." What a marvelous way to maintain and sustain unity in a body of solid believers! As the body, we need to help the church build walls of spiritual security that are safe from evil harm.

Below are simple ways we can support our Pastors in the church.

- Pray for them daily. 1 Thess 5:12–13, Col 4:2–4

- Encourage them with motivating words of grace and lovingkindness. Col 4:6, Heb 13:17

- Support them in their outreach ministry, locally and globally. Matt 28:19–20

- Pledge loyalty to their family for assistance when and where needed. 1 Tim 6:1–2

- Follow and be examples of their godly teaching in spreading the Good News.

    » Be godly listeners and doers of the Word. Jas 1:22–25, Eph 4:29

- Assist them in building up the Body of Christ by edifying others in the church while establishing unity. Eph chapter 4, Col 3:15–16, Rom 12:4–5

- Become a faithful and fruitful servant by performing our God-given gifts for a more significant cause for our Lord. 1 Pet 4:10–11, 1 Tim 4:14

- Exemplify ourselves as true representatives of Jesus Christ and the church through our daily actions, inside and outside His house. Col 3:17

- Provide for them financially so they can fulfill God's purpose and plan in the church and the Kingdom. Phil 4:18, 2 Cor chapter 9

- Allow and respect their time for rest. Mark 6:31

- Be full-time participants in the church, not part-timers.

    » Show genuine spiritual interest. Grow in faith, hope, and love. Heb 10:25, 1 Cor 3:9, Acts 2:46–47, Phil 2:2–3, 1 Cor chapter 13

- Be a blessing to their life. Gal 6:6, 1 Cor 10:31–33, 1 Tim 5:17

Ephesians chapter four is one of the most important chapters in the New Testament since the resurrection of Christ. Because within this chapter lies the foundation of the importance of our role in establishing the unity of the body of Christ as children of God—until His return. We are all one body and have a part to ensure that the body of Christ is safe, secured, and striving for His glory—not breaking down because of humans' expectations.

It starts with us abiding in our Lord, applying His word in our life, heeding the guidance of the Holy Spirit, supporting our pastor/leader, helping others, and living as His true representatives in and out of the church home. If we live by these basic principles, we, too, can help our pastors and leaders make an impact for God's Kingdom. We must realize that by working together as one in Christ, we can influence the Gospel and make a difference in this society and culture. Taking on this role as a godly influencer requires someone who is willing to accept it with "holy responsibility."

God desires and requires us to spread His word of love and grace throughout our communities, influencing people for Jesus Christ such as the Great Commission," Go out to all nations teaching and making disciples baptizing them in the name of the Father, Son, and Holy Spirit and teaching them to obey all the commands that were given to us." The Great Commission compels us to share the Good News until everyone has heard it. Then, like the servants in Jesus' parable, we are to be about the business of the kingdom, just like the Levites, making disciples of all nations—producing the fruit that God desires in our life.

You and I don't have to be prominent in the world's eyes to be influential people, especially since we have the same power of the indwelling Spirit to lead and guide us in teaching the truth of His Word. Through our example and life-changing testimonies, we can help others see and understand who Jesus Christ is and what it looks like to live for Him daily.

Scripture includes many examples of righteous men and women who were godly influencers in their generation. One of them was Daniel, a godly influence on his friends and kings that would span multiple kingdoms and personalities. Even as a youth, he was committed to obeying God's law. With that rooted faith and obedience, when Daniel was offered food from the Babylonian king's table, he requested foods that would comply with his Jewish dietary restrictions. His commitment to the Lord outweighed any fear of retaliation for rejecting the royal provisions of this earthly king. And because of Daniel's obedience, loyalty, and absolute faith, God protected him and showed him His favor when dealing with kings and kingdoms.

Although most of us will never get the opportunity to influence life globally, our Christlike examples can impact a workplace, church, neighborhood, people on the streets, home, or future generations. Just like Daniel, a godly example is rooted in obedience to Scripture because it's the source of wisdom. In a world of lawlessness, fear, and uncertainty, our confidence in the Lord stands out and influences those around us by how we do things in word and deed.

In Col 3:16–17, Paul reminds us, "Let the message about Christ, in all its richness, fill your lives. Teach and counsel each other with all the wisdom He gives. Sing psalms and hymns and spiritual songs to God with thankful hearts. And whatever you do or say, do it as a representative of the Lord Jesus, giving thanks through him to God the Father."

Just like the Levites were God's representatives throughout the nation of Israel and responsible for His children, as Christians today, whatever we do or say, let it be as a representative of Jesus Christ, our Lord. And when we live according to these words in the Bible, we bring honor and praise to His name in every aspect of our life. The impression of our Christian influence should be indicated in our homes, churches, neighborhood, and simply everywhere in life. Are we genuinely impacting God's Kingdom, leaving a trail of transformation that will alter people's lives around us?

We must remember, since the beginning of time, you and I have been given a job until the return of our Lord and Savior, Jesus Christ. Unfortunately, many Christians shun this duty and, most crucial calling because their mindset and heart do not regard our acts of service to God as a top priority. Ouch!

However, with today's rise of evilness, we must instill into the core fabric of our spiritual being, and God-fearing lives an essential responsibility that shows Who is reigning and governing our lives as servants. If we lean upon His empowering grace and strength, we can powerfully affect others around us.

We cannot influence others in a Christlike way if we're not close to our Lord. Only when the power of His word and Spirit is alive and at work in us can we take on this calling that will impact others in a positive and encouraging way. For us to move others in life-changing ways, we must rely on the strength of God, which will enable us to entice others in ways that will draw attention to Christ. When we insert more of His love, mercy, and grace into our Christian lives, that can influence someone's life at just the right time!

Matt 5:13–16, "You are the salt of the earth. But what good is salt if it has lost its flavor? Can you make it salty again? It will be thrown out and trampled underfoot as worthless. "You are the light of the world—like a city on a hilltop that cannot be hidden. No one lights a lamp and then puts it under a basket. Instead, a lamp is placed on a stand, where it gives light to everyone in the house. In the same way, let your good deeds shine out for all to see so that everyone will praise your heavenly Father."

CHAPTER 36

Godly Model

Num 36:1–3, 5–13, "Then the heads of the clans of Gilead—descendants of Makir, son of Manasseh, son of Joseph—came to Moses and the family leaders of Israel with a petition. They said, "Sir, the LORD instructed you to divide the land by sacred lot among the people of Israel. You were told by the LORD to give the grant of land owned by our brother Zelophehad to his daughters. But if they marry men from another tribe, their grants of land will go with them to the tribe into which they marry. In this way, the total area of our tribal land will be reduced…. So, Moses gave the Israelites this command from the LORD: "The claim of the men of the tribe of Joseph is legitimate. This is what the LORD commands concerning the daughters of Zelophehad: Let them marry anyone they like, as long as it is within their own ancestral tribe."

"None of the territorial land may pass from tribe to tribe, for all the land given to each tribe must remain within the tribe to which it was first allotted. The daughters throughout the tribes of Israel who are in line to inherit property must marry within their tribe so that all the Israelites will keep their ancestral property. No grant of land may pass from one tribe to another; each tribe of Israel must keep its allotted portion of land. The daughters of Zelophehad did as the LORD commanded Moses. Mahlah, Tirzah, Hoglah, Milcah, and Noah are all married cousins on their father's side. They married into the clans of Manasseh, son of Joseph. Thus, their inheritance of land remained within their ancestral tribe. These are the commands and regulations that the LORD gave to the people of Israel through Moses while they were camped on the plains of Moab beside the Jordan River, across from Jericho."

As we come to the end of the book of Numbers, it concludes with a compelling passage and storyline that involves how the land was to be distributed appropriately amongst the tribes. The intent was for the land to be kept within their lineages but also not to create division. This was a delicate matter that could only be addressed and handled with the guidance of God. And it involves five daughters who were not mentioned just once in God's word but five times. These women made their mark in the history of Jewish laws and not only caused a law to be changed for generations to come—but it was how they modeled themselves in their pursuit of change in a powerful and godly fashion.

This storyline is found in Numbers 27:1–7 when the daughters of Zelophehad, who had no brothers, came to Moses and the leaders asking for their fathers' possessions since he had died. The daughters of Zelophehad lived at the end of the Israelites' Exodus from Egypt as they prepared to enter the Promise Land. They were concerned about their inheritance, so they didn't sit idly by, allowing the status quo to determine their destiny.

As you read the passage closely in chapter twenty-seven, we see that their approach is one we should heed and model in our lives even today because their actions were honorable and memorable. As the daughters prepare to introduce their case, they approach Moses, the priest, and leaders using God's law as their means of solid support. They presented their case with clear facts and a posture of courage, humility, and respect, which is God-honoring and God-fearing.

As they presented their position, they did not complain and grumble like the Israelites who perished. Instead, they were steadfast with such faith and wisdom. And since this matter was uncommon, Moses asked God for direction, as we see in (Num 27:5–7). The Lord responded: "What Zelophehad's daughters are saying is legitimate. It would be best if you gave them a grant of land along with their father's relatives. Assign them the property that would have been given to their father"—God ruled in favor of the daughters!

The concern in the passage above in Chapter 36 was from the heads of the clan of Gilead, the tribe of Manasseh, the tribe Zelophehad belonged to. They told Moses that if the land was given to the daughters, then when they married, the land would go to their husband's tribe, and eventually, the original tribe's lands would become depleted.

So, the concern is not toward the women but for the continuity of the lines of inheritance within the tribes. Solving the problem of Zelophehad's daughters had created another problem within the nation: how to keep the property in a respective tribe throughout the generations. But Moses was given instructions from the Lord on how to divide up the land for inheritance in Num 26:52–56. The solution was simple; if a daughter in a family received an inheritance of land, she must marry within the tribe.

This phrase's repetition in verses seven and nine is for emphasis. If a daughter married outside the tribe, she had to forfeit the inheritance because the tribe had provisional rights, not only the individual. But how these five daughters approached this delicate situation with such godly wisdom, faith, and humility is an example we should live by in a society and culture that is emotionally amuck today. In any situation, using the foundation of God's word and led by the Holy Spirit should be foremost when urgent matters are approached. Even though the outcome may not turn out as you would like, the most important thing is that God is glorified and honored through the process.

As Christians, our #1 goal should be to conduct all personal and business affairs in honorable and pleasing ways to the Lord. How we model our lives as God-fearing and honoring Christ-followers should leave a mark of God-lasting memorable moments for His glory. And the most effective and biblical way is by imitating Christ in our daily lives. Is that difficult in today's time? Absolutely. But again, Peter reminds us in his second epistle in chapter one that we've been given every resource for living a godly life; in other words, there should be no excuse or moaning. Also, John reminds us in 1 John 5:3, "Loving God means keeping his commandments, and his commandments are not burdensome."

Our Lord never told us that obeying Him would come easy and without discomfort. Still, when we put our "all-out" efforts into applying His word, yielding to the Holy Spirit, and disciplining ourselves spiritually, our task as His representatives in any circumstance should never be burdensome or heavy for those who love the Lord! And we can attain that level of modeling our Lord and Savior only when we have a close and intimate relationship with Him.

When we have that close-knit bond with Christ, it impacts our internal motivations and desires, which in effect, demonstrates an external behavior that will always portray more of His model than just a mimic. Those who attempt to mimic our Lord and Savior do not possess His true character because they are phony and hypocrites. They are putting on a show out of their selfish desires, one that is not God-honoring.

An intimate and long-lasting relationship with the Lord is reflected in our submission, obedience, love, and faith and never wavering. And without these Christlike components in our lives, especially agape love, all our actions and attempts to be persuasive or impressive will mean nothing. The only mark and trail these types of people possess and leave are ones from a selfish and narcissistic perspective.

God expects you and me to demonstrate an everyday Christlike life that Jesus lived out when He walked upon this earth. He imitated and modeled His Heavenly Father perfectly in all His words and deeds. Will we be perfect in all our attempts? We all know the answer to this. We will always fall short of God's standards. However, the difference between authentic and fake Christians is that God's true children pursue His righteousness to avoid offending Him. And they set forth to model their lives morally and ethically, which are characteristics God desires in His children in their daily lifestyle, both in public and private. If only the Israelites had modeled this in their journey to the Promise Land.

God's nation of Israel's flaws in dishonoring and displeasing Him should be examples of how we should "not live" our Christian lives. We can accomplish ways that honor and please Him by following this passage in John 5:17–19, "But Jesus replied, "My Father is always working, and so am I." So, the Jewish leaders tried all the harder to find a way to kill him. He not only broke the Sabbath, he called God his Father, thereby making himself equal to God. So, Jesus explained, "I tell you the truth, the Son can do nothing by himself. He does only what he sees the Father doing. Whatever the Father does, the Son also does." In other words, whatever Christ modeled in His word, which honored His Father, is the life we should aim to live.

1 Cor 11:1, "And you should imitate me, just as I imitate Christ."

Eph 5:1–2, "Imitate God, therefore, in everything you do, because you are his dear children. Live a life filled with love, following the example of Christ. He loved us and offered himself as a sacrifice for us, a pleasing aroma to God."

Closing Comments

The message that we can ascertain from this all-embracing and timeless book is that it even reminds us of the spiritual warfare we are engaged in today. This fourth book in the Pentateuch is one of practical theology. It emphasizes the interaction between our Sovereign God and his people because it shows their dependence upon Him for daily guidance and His provisions.

The Book of Numbers portrays God as a God of structure and depicts His growth of order in Israel's society as a direct result of God's blessing. All the murmuring, grumbling, and rebellion were not new to God in this book, but what is apparent is God's discipline and judgment. God works with his people through this journey but holds them accountable for their actions.

God's reaction to Israel's rebellion was anger, leading to progressive measures for many who would lose their lives. Still, once again, God's mercy would come to the forefront when He provided a bronze snake lifted in their midst, accompanied by His instructions to look upon it and live—which required their steadfast faith in God's command.

This book in the Bible covers approximately 39 years, and it ends with the Israelites near the banks of the Jordan River, where they can see the Promise Land. They're finally going to make it. All the wandering is ending, and they are now preparing for their next big move based on God's commands. But as they looked across that river to the Promise Land, how many of them actually thought about everything they experienced to get to this point? They came this far by faith and will need even more confidence in God to take them the rest of the way.

From that early stage at Mount Sinai, God allowed Israel to grow from enslaved people—to "Promised Land" people. He taught them how to be ordered, organized, cleansed, separated, blessed, give, remember God's deliverance and promises, and provided them the tools to advance. They had been given everything needed to lean on the One who promised He would fulfill His word and provide a way for them to make it and be His blessed ones.

A central theological theme developed in the New Testament from Numbers is that sin and unbelief, especially rebellion and disobedience, reap the judgment of God. First Corinthians says explicitly—and Hebrews 3:7 and 4:13 strongly imply— that these events were written as examples for believers to observe and avoid. We are not to "set our hearts on evil things" (1 Cor 10:6), be sexually immoral (1 Cor 10:8), put God to the test (1 Cor 10:9), or gripe and complain (1 Cor 10:10).

Just as the Israelites wandered in the wilderness for forty years because of their rebellion, so does God sometimes allow us to wander away from Him and suffer loneliness and lack of blessings when we rebel against Him. But God is faithful and just. He restored the Israelites to their rightful place in His heart. And He will always restore Christians to the place of blessing and intimate fellowship with Him if we repent and return to Him (1 John 1:9). While the wandering wilderness could be due to rebellion and sin in our lives, it most importantly will reveal God's grace and provisions.

Unfortunately, Christians die in their wilderness because they will not trust God or enter the promises He has set before them. And this lack of faith will succumb because of the weakness of their flesh. And sadly, many Christians live more in the wilderness than on the threshold of His Promised Land.

The wilderness is an unpleasant place, fleshly speaking, and we naturally want prosperity, health, and an easy-going life. But the same God who created the perfect garden also created the wilderness. There will be times of trial and pressure in our daily life, and our faith will be tested. But the God of grace will meet us even in the wilderness and set the ones with a willing, faithful, obedient, humble, and contrite heart on His path of righteousness and goodness!

As God's creation, we all matter in the eyes of our Heavenly Creator. He wants us to be "counted as His own" and wants to ensure that our lives possess the connecting Dots back to His Son, our Savior, Jesus Christ. However, He will not tolerate unrepentant sin and continued disobedience in our lives. If we want to be included in His heavenly census, our choice will come down to each of us; He will not force us to choose. As Creator, He cares enough to include us—but we must care enough to follow His ways obediently and faithfully.

Psalm chapter 139 reminds us, "O LORD, you have examined my heart and know everything about me. You know when I sit down or stand up. You know my thoughts even when I'm far away. You see me when I travel and when I rest at home. You know everything I do. You know what I am going to say even before I say it, LORD. You go before me and follow me. You place your hand of blessing on my head. Such knowledge is too wonderful for me, too great for me to understand! I can never escape from your Spirit! I can never get away from your presence! If I go up to heaven, you are there; if I go down to the grave, you are there. If I ride the wings of the morning, if I dwell by the farthest oceans, even there, your hand will guide me, and your strength will support me. I could ask the darkness to hide me and the light around me to become night—but even in darkness, I cannot hide from you. To you, the night shines as bright as day. Darkness and light are the same to you. You made all the delicate, inner parts of my body and knit me together in my mother's womb. Thank you for making me so wonderfully complex! Your workmanship is marvelous—how well I know it. You watched me as I was being formed in utter seclusion, as I was woven together in the dark of the womb. You saw me before I was born. Every day of my life was recorded in your book. Every moment was laid out before a single day had passed. How precious are your thoughts about me, O God. They cannot be numbered! I can't even count them; they outnumber the grains of sand! And when I wake up, you are still with me! O God, if only you would destroy the wicked! Get out of my life, you murderers! They blaspheme you; your enemies misuse your name. O LORD, shouldn't I hate those who hate you? Shouldn't I despise those who oppose you? Yes, I hate them with total hatred, for your enemies are my enemies. Search me, O God, and know my heart; test me and know my anxious thoughts. Point out anything in me that offends you and lead me along the path of everlasting life."

Bibliography

Delony, John. "The Importance of Human Connection." Ramsey, May 31, 2023. https://www.ramseysolutions.com/relationships/importance-of-human-connection.

"Doctrine of Balaam." Got Questions Ministry. https://www.gotquestions.org/doctrineofBalaam.html.

Fairchild, Mary. "Cleanliness is Next to Godliness and the Bible." Learn Religions, September 1, 2020. https://www.learnreligions.com/cleanliness-is-next-to-godliness bible.html.

"Fifty Christian Quotes to Inspire Your Faith Every Day." Crosswalk Ministry. https://www.crosswalk.com/faith/spiritual-life/inspiring-quotes/30-inspiring-christian-quotes.

Francisco, Erick Brent. "Safety Culture. A Guide to Good Distribution." February 17, 2023. https://safetyculture.com/topics/good-distribution-practice-gdp.

Graham, Billy. "Does God Give Us Second Chances." Answers Devotions, June 27, 2017. https://billygraham.org/answer/does-god-give-us-second-chances.

Hanson, Dana. "The Twenty Worst Prisons in America." Money Inc., March 29, 2023. https://moneyinc.com/worst-prisons-in-america.

Healey, Jennifer. "23 Quotes about Darkness and Light to Help You Appreciate Both." Healing Brave Journal, July 1, 2016. https://healingbrave.com/blogs/all/quotes-about-darkness-and-light.

Stanley, Charles. "Blessed to Bless Others." In Touch Ministries, March 31, 2022. https://www.intouch.org/read/daily-devotions/blessed-to-bless-others.

Lamoureux, Tammy. "Thirty-Seven Christian Leadership Quotes." March 10, 2015. https://www.curatedquotes.com/leadership-quotes/christian.

"Numbers 5— Separating from Sin." Enduring Word Ministry. https://enduringword.com/bible-commentary/numbers-5/.

"Numbers 12— The Dissension of Aaron and Miriam." Enduring Word Ministry. https://enduringword.com/bible-commentary/numbers-12.

"Numbers 15— Various Laws and Provision." Enduring Word Ministry. https://enduringword.com/bible.commentary/numbers-15

"Numbers 18—Laws Pertaining to Priests and Levites." Enduring Word Ministry. https://enduringword.com/bible-commentary/numbers-18.

"Numbers 19— The Red Heifer and the Cleansing Waters." Enduring Word Ministry. https://enduringword.com/bible-commentary/numbers-19.

"Numbers 21—On the Way to Canaan." Enduring Word Ministry. https://enduringword.com/bible commentary/numbers-21.

"Numbers 24— The Prophecies of Balaam." Enduring Word Ministry. https://enduringword.com/bible-commentary/numbers-24.

"Numbers 28—Sacrifices for Appointed Days and Feasts." Enduring Word Ministry. https://enduringword.com/bible-commentary/numbers-28.

"Numbers 32— The Tribes Settling East of Jordan." Enduring Word Ministry. https://enduringword.com/bible-commentary/numbers-32.

"Numbers 30— The Keeping of Vows." Enduring Word Ministry. https://enduringword.com/bible-commentary/numbers-30.

"Numbers 31— Vengeance on Midian." Enduring Word Ministry. https://enduringword.com/bible-commentary/numbers-31.

The Ethics and Religious Livery Commission of the Southern Baptist Convention. "Inspiring Stories of God's Power in the Lives of Ordinary Men." February 28, 2020. https://erlc.com/resource-library/articles/inspiring-stories-of-gods-power-in-the-lives-of-ordinary-men.

"What Are Boundaries and Are they Biblical." Got Questions Ministry. https://www.gotquestions.org/boundaries-biblical.html.

"What Are Practical Ways to Depend on God Alone." Got Questions Ministry. https://www.gotquestions.org/depend-on-God.html.

"What Did Jesus Mean When He Said. "I Am the True Vine." Got Questions Ministry. https://www.gotquestions.org/true-vine.html.

"What Does the Bible Say About Second Chances." Got Questions Ministry. https://www.gotquestions.org/second-chances.html.

"What is the Favor of God and How Can I Get It?" Got Questions Ministry. https://www.gotquestions.org/favor-of-God.html.

"What Does it Mean to Taste and See that the Lord is Good. Psalm 34:8?" Got Questions Ministry. https://www.gotquestions.org/taste-see-Lord-good.html.

"What Does it Mean that We Are a Royal Priesthood." Got Questions Ministry. https://www.gotquestions.org/royal-priesthood.html.

"What is the Key to Bearing Fruit as a Christian." Got Questions Ministry. https://www.gotquestions.org/bearing-fruit.html.

"What is the Land that God Promised to Israel." Got Questions Ministry. https://www.gotquestions.org/Israel-land.html.

"What Principles Should Distinguish a Christians Business." Got Questions Ministry. https://www.gotquestions.org/Christian-business.html.

"What the Bible Says About Communication." Got Questions Ministry. https://www.gotquestions.org/Bible-communication.html.

"Why Did God Choose Me." Got Questions Ministry. https://www.gotquestions.org/why-did-God choose-me.html.

Glossary

A

Abandoned — deserted, forsaken, cast aside, unused, *but you are never stranded in Christ!*

Able — *capable and qualified to have the power, skill, and means to work for the Lord!*

Abundance — large quantity, mass, *extremely abundant life as a believer in Jesus.*

Acceptance — receive something suitable, approved, *welcoming His Word in your life.*

Access —a means of entering a place - *your entrance into Heaven as a believer in Christ.*

Accomplish —achieve, complete, fulfill, finish, and conclude *our victory in Jesus Christ.*

Accountable —responsible, bound to, liable, *we are to blame and will be held!*

Accused —charged with a crime, charges against the guilty, *but in Christ, you are innocent.*

Acknowledge —*accept the truth of God's word, bow to it, and address it in your life.*

Action —doing something, aim towards, *steps and efforts taken to know our Lord more.*

Admit —*acknowledge, profess, and confess that Jesus Christ is Lord of your life.*

Advantage —*once we surrender to Christ — there's new life in Him, sins forgiven, transformed, power of His indwelling Spirit at work in us, faithful servants, eternal life.*

Advice —*guidance, recommendation, direction, and pointers provided in God's word.*

Affection —*a gentle fondness of love, endearment, and friendship we can have with Christ.*

Agape Love —the highest form of love, *the love of God for man, and of man for God.*

Agreement —*in harmony, accordance, and agreeing with God's ways in your life.*

Aim —*work towards, set sights on, pursue, strive for, and target Christlikeness.*

Alert —readiness for action, *discerning towards a threat or danger that could be harmful.*

Align —*arrange your life in an order that positions and sets you toward Christlikeness.*

Alliance —*a union for mutual benefit, a bonded association with Christ in your life.*

Almighty —absolute overall and unlimited Power in all things —*nothing compares to God.*

Allows —approve of, pleased with, invest, entrust, *yield to, and acknowledge His ways.*

Alone —the state of no one present in your life, singleness. *But as Christians, we know that He's always there.*

Alter —is a structure upon which offerings such as sacrifices are made for religious purposes—a place for consecration. *Our hearts are an invisible altar where the war between the flesh and the spirit rages. When we surrender areas of our lives to the control of the Holy Spirit, we are, in effect, laying that area on the altar before God.*

Alternative —*available as another opportunity of relief, like accepting Christ as Savior.*

Ambition —a fervent desire to achieve something, intention, purpose, *a goal to serve God.*

Anew —a new, different, and typically more positive way, *a fresh new beginning in Him.*

Anger —a strong feeling of hostility and rage, *but in Christ, He can provide self—control.*

Ambition —a powerful desire to achieve something, *an intent to know and grow in Christ.*

Anointed —chosen for a position, and *once in Christ, you are His candidate for service.*

Anxiety —is a reaction to a stressful situation, but God's word comforts us.

Apart —separated away from, distant, far away, *cut off, let go for good — done.*

Apostasy —the abandonment, betrayal, defection, and desertion of faith — *spiritual doom.*

Apparent —clearly visible, understood, plain, striking, recognizable, *manifest Godliness.*

Apply —make an effort, use, exercise, put into practice, and *show commitment to His word.*

Appointed —specified, determined, allotted, assigned, *designated, chosen for His glory.*

Approval —to be honest and trustworthy, having a positive and *favorable opinion of Him in us.*

Arrogance —attitude of superiority, *extreme sense of one's importance, spiritually weak.*

Ashamed —embarrassed, guilty because of an action, *one choice for Christ removes it all.*

Ask —*call for,* seek for His counsel, beg, and *crave for His direction and guidance.*

Assumption —accepted as accurate without proof, *God's word is precept upon precept.*

Atonement —*restitution, satisfying a wrongdoing, reconciling with God through Jesus.*

Attempt —do your best, strive, make every effort, and give your *all to the Lord.*

Attention —*take notice, away, observe, regard as in paying attention to the Scripture.*

Attitude —way of thinking, perspective, approach, your feelings — *good or bad?*

Authority —*the power of the right to give orders in our life, such as God's word in us.*

Awe —*reverential respect, admiration, wonder, and amazement in all God has done!*

B

Balance —*stability, steadiness, and footing in daily life, such as God's word at work.*

Barren —too poor to produce, unfruitful, *but fruitfulness can be abundant in Christ.*

Barrier —an obstacle that prevents movement or access, a hurdle, *a spiritual roadblock.*

Basics —*the essential facts, principles, and realities of God's word active in us daily.*

Behavior —one's conduct, actions, practices, manners, ways, *habits — pure or impure?*

Benefit —*an advantage or profit gained, such as our eternal inheritance in Christ.*

Bind —*tied, fastened together, shackled, and secured in Christ once we believe in Him.*

Bitterness —*anger and resentment that can be removed once a believer in Christ.*

Blame —*one held accountable, condemnation, accused, but in Christ, you're forgiven.*

Blameless —innocent of wrongdoing, free from blame, *faultless in God's eyes as His.*

Blasphemy —the unforgivable sin, ungodliness, disrespect, unholy, *but the Lord forgives.*

Belief —an acceptance that a statement is true, *free from doubt in who you are in Christ.*

Believer —one who believes *something is effective, a follower and disciple of Christ.*

Birth – *Spiritual —one who has been born into the family of God and craves fellowship with other believers — and a desire to grow, develop and mature in Christlikeness.*

Blessed —our well-being and *the full impact of God's presence in our lives.*

Blessings —*God's favor, goodness, goodwill, and happiness in our lives.*

Blindness —poor perception, *inability to see anything spiritually impure or hurtful.*

Blood of Christ —*sacrificial death and complete atoning work of Jesus on our behalf.*

Boasting —excessively proud, self-satisfied about oneself – *no place in God's house.*

Body of Christ —*collection and unity of true believers in a place of service and praising Christ.*

Boldness —willingness – the quality of a solid and clear appearance, *fearless for God.*

Breath of Life —the life and power of God, given to man to operate him, get him going, set him in motion, but the key lies in this – *who controls our on and off button?*

Burdensome —challenging to carry out or fulfill; only *with God's help can we persevere.*

Business of God —*managing and stewardship of God's ways for His purpose and plan.*

Busyness —many things to do *that can lead to a disconnection from God.*

C

Calamity —an event causing significant distress, affliction, crisis, adversity, or *temporary setback.*

Calculating —scheming, ruthless behavior, self-interest, *driven by the flesh than spirit.*

Calling —a strong urge toward a particular way of life, mission, or *course of action for God.*

Callous —insensitive, cruel disregard for others, cold-hearted, the heart of stone, *not of God.*

Carelessness —failure to give *attention to God* in an area that could avoid harm or errors.

Caring —*a kindhearted and genuine concern for all people in a Christlike fashion.*

Chance —the possibility of something happening, *an opportunity, and hope to make it right.*

Change —different, converted, transformed, *a Godly make-over for His glory.*

Character —personality, attributes, *identity, qualities, the uniqueness of Christ in us.*

Choice —select, decide, option, course of action, solution, *way out from the bad to good.*

Chosen —*selected, fitting, suitable, called for, expected, preferred by God for His glory.*

Christian —*one who believes in, professes, and follows all the ways of Jesus Christ.*

Christianity —*belief in the teachings of Christ's life, death, and resurrection, Good News.*

Christlike —the result of Christian growth and maturity, *exemplifying behaviors of Christ.*

Church —*The Body* — *all who have placed their faith in Jesus Christ for salvation.*

Citizenship —*citizens of Heaven on earth with our eternal resting place in His Kingdom.*

Clarity —apparent, simple, plain, understandable; *there is no confusion in God's word. It's crystal clear.*

Cleansing —intent to clean something thoroughly, purify *Christ, can wash away our sins.*

Cling —grasp, clench, grip, hold onto "tightly" *all of God's ways for your life.*

Clothing *Spiritually* —indicates spiritual character developed by submission to God. *Christians are to "put on the Lord Jesus Christ " like a garment representing a Christ—covered life and, as a result, character consistent with God's way of life.*

Comfort —a state of ease, freedom from pain, *a reassurance of God's peace in us.*

Comfort Zone —behavioral state of anxiety control, *lack of spiritual growth.*

Command —authoritative order, instruct, charge, *require, prescribed from God.*

Commitment —*dedicated, devoted, faithful, attentive to a cause for our good — His glory.*

Communication —*God communicates to us through His word, and we talk to Him in prayer.*

Community —*a body that loves Jesus Christ and fellowships and supports each other.*

Communion —*sharing intimate thoughts, remembering what Christ did for us.*

Compare —contrast, differentiates —the difference between, side by side, *flesh vs. spirit?*

Compelled —forced, pressured, or *an obligation to do something like living out His word.*

Complacent —self-satisfied, proud, pleased with self, careless, lazy, *spiritually flawed.*

Complainer —dissatisfaction, grumbler, moaner, whiner, find fault, *spiritually toxic.*

Completion —*the fulfillment, fruition, and his successful work in us until Glory.*

Compromise —agreement, settled, trade-off, cooperate, give-and-take— *God or world?*

Condemnation —extreme disapproval of, *but there is no condemnation if you belong to Jesus Christ.*

Confessions —admitting guilt, owning up, being accountable, professing, exposing, *a Godly act.*

Confidence —a belief that we can rely on another, *a firm trust like our position with Christ.*

Confirm —*establish correctness,* discover, determine, grasp, take in, and *cling to His Truths.*

Conflict —a dispute that can lead to discord and division —*so often, it is the work of Satan.*

Conform —comply with rules, abide by, obey, agree to, fulfill, respect, and *stick to God.*

Confusion —*lack of understanding,* uncertainty, doubt, hesitancy, *the enemy at work.*

Connection —relationship, *linked together, relevant, relatable, bonded with the Lord.*

Conscience is awareness and knowledge of right and wrong; the *key for believers is applying God's word.*

Consecrate —*as true believers; our lives are a living sacrifice to Him, separated from evil.*

Consequences —a result or effect of an action or outcome *could be dire.*

Consistent —*done the same way over time, accurate, no variation from God's word.*

Consuming —devour, take, feast on, engaging, deeply felt, *filling our minds with Him.*

Contentment —happiness, satisfaction, pleasure, comfort, *gratified with His provisions.*

Contrary —opposite and inconsistent, *such as the ways of the world vs. God's ways.*

Contrast —*strikingly different; as believers in Christ, we are unlike anything in this world.*

Conversation —a talk between people the Lord welcomes from us daily.

Conviction —declaring someone guilty, *a position that can be made right once in Christ.*

Cooperate —work jointly towards the same result *with God every day.*

Correction —making something right, rectifying, *all cleared up when we accept Christ!*

Corruption —dishonesty, deception, wrongdoing, *misconduct that is not a life in Christ.*

Counsel —advice, guidance, direction, *enlightenment facts from His Spirit for our good.*

Covenant —a binding agreement, a *life-or-death agreement between two — you and God.*

Craftsmen —God gives talent and ability to specific individuals to carry out His work to its completion. *To conduct His designs with success and* an element of excellence and success in their works; we all have that capacity through the Holy Spirit.

Creation —completeness, totality, fulfillment, or perfection – *God's awesomeness.*

Creator —Someone Who brings something *into existence and sustains it— God at work.*

Credibility —trustworthy, character, dependable, *reputation of a Godly person.*

Cross —*the intersection of God's love and His justice. For believers in Christ's sacrifice, it's being dead to self and following Jesus wholeheartedly.*

Crown —*an honor received for our good and faithful works and a cause for boundless joy.*

Crucial —critical to the success or failure of something, significant, *game-changer.*

Cunning —having skill in achieving one's end; deceptive, crafty, *scheming, not good.*

Curtain —divided the two sacred rooms of the Tabernacle — the Holy Place and Most Holy Place. It symbolizes how people were separated from God because of sin. Thanks to Christ, this curtain has been ripped, and we now have access to the Father because of what Christ did for us on the cross.

D

Danger —the possibility of suffering or harm, hazard, risk, or *instability when not in Christ.*

Darkness —partial or total absence of light, gloom, *dullness, void, and blackness.*

Death —the end of physical life, *but as believers in Christ, spiritual life continues forever.*

Deceive —causing one to believe *what is untrue, mislead, fool, cheat, double-crosser.*

Decision —a resolution, settled, and *final when you accept Christ as Lord.*

Declines —refuse to take advantage of, turn down, pass up, *could change your life.*

Dedication is setting apart or consecrating things to God, devoted to a holy purpose by a Divine Being.

Defiance —open resistance, bold disobedience, *disregard, rebellious —be careful.*

Delight —*please someone significantly, what the Lord desires from us daily.*

Delivered —the deliverance of God's people from sin and guilt, God's supremacy over the Egyptian deities.

Demand —insistent request, an order, ultimatum, urge, stipulation, *challenge to get right.*

Demonstrate —show how something is done, display, illustrate, and *exemplify His qualities.*

Depend —*controlled by, rely on, be based on, rest, and lean on God for all things.*

Depraved —corrupt, wicked, lead astray, poison another, defile, infect – *not of God.*

Desires —want, yearning, longing, craving, *eagerness, enthusiasm to know God more.*

Despair —*complete loss or absence of hope,* unhappiness, discouragement, depression.

Desperate —feeling hopeless at one's end, *but not in Christ, for you are anew.*

Destroy —put an end to, damage, tear down, break up, devastate, *enemy's goal.*

Determined —made a firm decision, resolved *not to change when you accept Christ.*

Develop —form, grow, more mature, *flourish, blossom, succeed in all His ways.*

Devise —think up, develop, formulate, design, and *plan to know God more.*

Devour —consume, gorge oneself, gobble up — *things we should do with God's word.*

Difficult —need effort and skill to achieve, weary, brutal, *without God's —it is impossible.*

Diligence —persistent effort, attention to detail, continuance, *an intent to please Him.*

Disadvantage —*an unfavorable circumstance, a defect, or a liability that could be costly.*

Disagree —a different opinion, fail to agree, challenge, argue, quarrel, *be careful.*

Discernment —*God-gifted ability to judge well, wise, sharp, insightful, so needed today.*

Discontent —dissatisfaction, lack of contentment, a sense of grievance; it's *spiritually crippling.*

Discourage —cause someone to lose confidence, enthusiasm, *not a Christlike attribute.*

Disobedience —failure or refusal to obey rules or God's authority.

Distract —prevent from giving full attention to something. It's a state of disturbance and confusion; it's the *devil's work.*

Disposition— *"Spiritually"* —*how we respond to life and, most importantly, God. Our response to Him should be essential in our minds daily.*

Divine —*Godly, Godlike, Saintly, Spiritual, Heavenly, Holy; it's God's ways.*

Division —the act of separating, breaking up, splitting, severing, *disconnecting from the bad to good.*

Doer —*takes an active part, does not just think about it, "achieving God's directives."*

Doubt —connotes the idea of weakness in faith, negative attitude, or action — *not of God.*

E

Effective —successful in producing the desired result, valuable, *such as our walk with God.*

Effort —a vigorous or determined attempt, endeavor, an *all-out exertion to serve Him.*

Elevate —*raise and lift up that higher position you possess in Christ — every day.*

Embrace —hold closely in one's arms, clasp to, enclose, and *entwine oneself around the Lord.*

Emotions —a natural state of mind, feeling, sensation, *reaction or response, passion for?*

Emptiness —contain nothing, worthless, ineffective, *once wholly in Christ— you are filled.*

Encourage —*supporter, confidence or hope to one, uplift, helpful, a Christlike enforcer.*

Endurance —tolerance, bearing, patience, acceptance, persistence, *a staying power in Him.*

Engage —become involved, participate in, embark on, and *play a key role in all His ways.*

Enhance —*intensify, increase, and further improve the quality of your walk with the Lord.*

Enlightenment —learning, development, insight, *and advancement in God's ways.*

Enslaved —a cause to someone losing their freedom of choice or action. Christ can release us from any bondage and give us freedom forever when He chooses life in Him.

Enthusiasm —intense and eager enjoyment, *nothing like a relationship with Jesus Christ.*

Envy —jealousy, covet, bitterness, resentment, a wrong desire, *a sinful vice that cripples.*

Equality —a state of being equal, *fair, and impartial;* we *are all created by God equally.*

Error —a mistake, oversight, misinterpretation, *a misconception, but God can fix it.*

Establish —set up, start, begin, get going, and *bring into being your intended life for Him.*

Everlasting —forever, without end, imperishable, immortal, deathless – *priceless.*

Evidence —proof, confirms, reveals, displays, manifests, and *signifies your identity in Christ.*

Evil —wicked, harmful, corrupt, immoral, sin —*life or death matter.*

Exalt —hold someone in high regard, *glorify, praise, worship, and reverence to the Holy One.*

Example —*characteristic of its kind, illustrating one's case, a representative for Christ.*

Excitement —a *feeling of great enthusiasm and eagerness as you grow closer to the Lord.*

Exclusive —complete, total, whole, absolute, *your undivided attention to the Lord.*

Excuse —seek to justify, rationalize, overlook, disregard, or *ignore the Good News.*

Exodus —a mass departure of people, God's great deliverance for His children in bondage.

Expectation —the belief that something will happen, anticipation, the *outlook for our good.*

Experience —valuable contact, acquaintance, exposure to, and *understanding of Him in you.*

F

Failure —lack of success, unfulfilling, *but as a true child of God, you have not failed.*

Faith —complete trust, confidence, hopefulness, belief, *dependence upon His word.*

Faithfulness —unfailing loyalty to someone, *consistently putting into practice His ways.*

Faithless —disloyal, unfaithful, unreliable, *even though we are faithless, God's faithful.*

Fatalism —the belief that all events are inevitable *and out of God's control. It debilitates faith.*

Favor —gaining approval, acceptance, pleasure, or *unique benefits or blessings from Him.*

Fear —terror, alarm, anxiety, worry, uneasiness, distress, doubt, dread, *spiritual weakness.*

Feel —awareness, sense, discern, *conscious of something powerful at work in us.*

Find —discover, realize, become aware, appear, show, and *manifest His word in us.*

Fixated —*obsessed with, gripped by, devoted to, focused — as we should be as* Christians.

Flee —run away from danger, escape, leave, get out quickly, *spiritually discerning.*

Flesh —*the part of a believer who disagrees with the Spirit — cannot coexist.*

Filth —foul, disgusting dirt, contamination, and garbage—is *not a spiritual virtue.*

Focus —the *center of interest, focal point, backbone, anchor,* the *basis of the Controlling One in our lives.*

Follower —*a devoted person to a cause, companion, admirer, supporter, lover of Christ.*

Fool —acting unwisely, imprudent, idiot, *a halfwit not taking God's word seriously.*

Foothold —*an issue of who influences the heart. Is it the Lord or the enemy? A place where you can put your foot safely and securely when climbing like the Rock.*

Footstool —is a symbol of lowliness, humility, and unimportance—*selflessness.*

Forgetfulness —lose the remembrance of, forget facts; God's *word is a fresh reminder daily.*

Forgiveness —absolute forgiving, cleared, pardon, *God's mercy on us as sinners.*

Foundation —starting point, heart, principle, fundamentals, cornerstone, *Godly position.*

Freedom —*the power, right, and privilege we possess to speak of the Good News of Christ.*

Fruit of the Spirit —*Holy Spirit's presence, working in the lives of true maturing believers.*

Fruitfulness —*is beneficial for the work of the Lord in our daily lives for His Glory.*

Fulfill —bring to completion, succeed, and *bring about His good fruit in your daily life.*

GLOSSARY

Futile —incapable of producing valid results, pointless, *but His Spirit in us can have.*

G

Genealogy —historical facts in the Bible, the importance of family to God, proof of prophecies.

Generosity is the Christlike quality of genuine kindness, honor, and lack of *prejudice.*

Gentleness —*supreme kindness, mild-mannered, tender, softness, courteous, considerate.*

Genuine —someone authentic, honest, legit, sound, sterling, *rightful in all His ways.*

Gifts —given willingly, a present, offering, favor, inheritance, *bestowal from Him to us.*

Giving —handing over freely, *God's children providing others with what He is gifted us.*

Glorify —praise, exalt, worship, reverence, adore, honor, bless, *magnify Him in all we do.*

Glory —*splendor, holiness, and majesty of God, a place of unfathomable praise and honor.*

Goal —a future desired result to achieve something *as Citizens of Heaven on Earth.*

God —*All Supreme Being, Creator, Who is Perfect in Power, Wisdom, and Goodness.*

Godly Fear —*a reverent feeling to God, a deterrent to sin, and brings us closer to God.*

God's Fairness —*living under God's righteousness and justness — love, grace, and mercy.*

God's Kingdom —the rule of an eternal, sovereign God over all the universe.

God's Laws —His unchangeable divine nature, expression of love, joy, holy, just, pleasing.

God's Nature —*All Supreme — Holy, Just, Righteous, All Omni, Loving Kind Creator.*

God's Presence —*always present in believers by His Spirit*— a strong relationship.

God's Promises —*to help strengthen our faith* and have something to hold on to.

God's Protection —*Heaven is our home—we are spiritually safe as believers in Christ.*

God's Season —*appointed time for all seasons of life* — *part of living out God's plan.*

God's Timing —*when all falls comfortably, naturally into place* — *in His appointed time.*

God's View —*God always sees how everything works together to conform us to His image.*

God's Will is things that align *with God's superior and supreme plan and purpose.*

God's Word —the infallible *Truth, Righteous, and Goodness of all God's Holy ways.*

God's Work —*where we are equipped with His gift to benefit others and accomplish His good works in love and faithfulness* — *with His guidance* — *representing Him.*

Godliness —*the practice, exercise, and discipline of devoutness to God's word.*

Good —satisfactory, acceptable, high quality, and standard, *up to His mark.*

Goodness —*Godly virtue, integrity, honesty, truthfulness, honorable, righteousness, caring.*

Gossiper —betrayal of confidence, a perverse person stirring up dissension, *not Godly.*

Grace —*God's favor towards the unworthy, His goodwill, generosity, and lovingkindness.*

Gratitude —*the Godly quality of thankfulness, appreciation, recognition, credit, and respect.*

Greed —a selfish desire for something, most often worldly things — *not God.*

Growth —*the increasing, maturing, thriving, and sprouting of Christlikeness in us.*

Guide — *"One" who shows the way to others and gives advice to resolve life's problems.*

Guilt —committed a crime or wrongdoing but *cleared when accepting Christ as Savior.*

H

Habits —a regular practice or custom that is hard to give up, *maybe a spiritual detriment.*

Half—heartedness —no enthusiasm or energy, *not "all in" — wholeheartedly for the Lord.*

Happiness —the feeling of joy and satisfaction that *we should experience daily as Christians.*

Hardheartedness —incapable of being moved to pity or tenderness, *no Christlike value.*

Harmony —in tune simultaneously, sounds *joined into whole units—as one.*

Harvest—*Spiritual —users of our gifts in God's field to reap what we sow, a sign of growth.*

Hatred —intense dislike or ill will, *a poison that can destroy our spirit from within.*

Healing —the process of becoming sound or healthy – *spiritually eased and relieved.*

Health —*a continual spiritual treatment and nourishment of our heart, mind, and soul.*

Heaven —physical reality beyond earth—*the spiritual reality where God lives, where we can also live as believers in Jesus Christ—forever.*

Heavenly Father —First person of the Trinity – *Supreme Being, Creator, and Sustainer.*

Hear —get, listen to, *discern, be informed,* told, made aware of, *given to understand Him.*

Heart —*the central part and core of our spiritual makeup in thoughts, actions, and words.*

Heart Set —*modeling the force of what is controlling the heart to the outside world! It is either glorifying God or not.*

Heed —pay attention to take notice of, consider, *give ear to observe, and apply His ways.*

Hell —the total, conscious, eternal separation from God's blessings, *so choose Christ.*

Helper —one that helps, aids, or assists, *a Christlike assistant out of genuine love.*

Holiness is God's most divine nature and characteristic, which is the goal of all human moral character. It is a disposition of being separate from the ways of the world and required to be in God's Almighty presence.

Holy Spirit —the third person of the Trinity, Comforter, Counselor — *God in action in our life.*

Honesty —*moral correctness, high principles, right-mindedness, worthiness, Godly truth.*

Honor —high respect, esteem, distinction, privilege, respect, *notable to the True God.*

Hope —expectation for a sure thing to happen, *longing for a great outcome.*

Hopelessness —absolute despair, no hope, a feeling of loss, but hope is alive and well in Christ.

Hospitality —the *Christlike quality* of friendly and *generous reception of all people.*

Humility —*Christlike modesty, a low view of oneself, lack of pride, Godly meekness.*

I

Idolatry —*worship of idols other than God, ungodliness, and unholy in the eyes of God.*

Ignore —refuse to notice, *disregard, leave out, disobey, defy.* [insert sad face]

Image —a representation of the external form, likeness, resemblance, portrayal – *Godly.*

Imitator —one who copies the behavior of another, a person *in high esteem — Jesus Christ.*

Immaturity —not growing, *a "spiritual infant" looks and acts like a human infant.*

Immoral —not conforming or accepting standards of morality, *spiritual lostness.*

Immortal —*living forever, never dying or decaying for those in Jesus Christ.*

Impact —a substantial effect on others, highly influential, *make an impression for His glory.*

Impartial —treating everyone fairly and equally, *leaving all doors open as God does.*

Impatience —no patience, irritable, restless, *complete opposite of the Fruit of the Spirit.*

Imperative —necessary, mandatory, pressing, urgent, *could be dire — if not a Believer.*

Important —significant value, an effect on success, *like living out God's word daily.*

Impression —a feeling or opinion about someone, view, perception, the *image of Him in us.*

Impulsive —done without forethought, in many, if not all cases, *no spiritual discernment.*

Inclusive —*all around, all-embracing, and all in for the Lord —without hesitation.*

Indifference —lack of concern, interest, or sympathy, no feelings, *distant from Godliness.*

Incense *Spiritual* —are the things of worship that are *acceptably* perceived, such as confessions, adorations, and prayers — things from the thought and mouth that bear relation to the truths of faith.

Influencer —*the power and impact we have on others when God's word is thriving in us.*

Initiative —*ambition, motivation, and drive to assess God's word and move forward.*

Insecure —unstable, weak, *not firmly fixed or grounded in the blanket of God's security.*

Insensitive —showing no feelings for others, callous, *lacking God's guidance.*

Instructions —order, command, directive, requirement, *stipulations given in His word.*

Integrity —*Christlike quality of moral uprightness, high principles in line with God.*

Interests —wanting to learn more about something, attentive, *honest students of God's word.*

Intentional —done on purpose, deliberate, thought out, *knowingly pleasing Him daily.*

Intercessor —is someone who prays, petitions, or begs God in favor of another person. Jesus Christ is our Intercessor!

Interpret —explain the meaning of, *make clear, understand, and resolve for our good purpose.*

J

Jealousy —discontent, resentment, *it means we are not happy with what God's given us.*

Jesus Christ —*God incarnate, the second person of the Trinity, Lord, Redeemer, Messiah, King, Savior, Son of the Living God, Creator, Wonderful Counsellor, Righteous One, Bread of Life, Advocate, Lamb of God, Good Shepherd, Bridegroom, Son of Man, Alpha and Omega, The Way, Truth, and Life.*

Joined —fixed together, connected, attached, *yoked, chained, locked in with Him.*

Journey —the act of moving, *making one's way down God's path of Righteousness.*

Joy —*greatest of pleasures,* happiness, delight, *rejoicing, and exultation of our life in Christ.*

Judgment—Final —*unbelievers are judged for their sins and cast into eternal separation.* [insert sad face]

Judging —*determine the biblical act of righteous and unrighteous behavior in a believer.*

Justice —is rooted in the very nature of God as a Righteous Judge. He rewards good, and he does not ignore the sins of any; He renders to everyone what is due, which means we are held accountable.

Justified —*declared righteous because of our faith in what Christ did for us on the cross.*

K

Kindness —a *great concern for all, expecting nothing in return, genuine Godly sincerity.*

Knowing —realize, aware, understand, sense, recognize, *notice right from wrong.*

Knowledge —comprehend, mastered, accomplishment, intelligence, *God's insight.*

L

Lawlessness is the stage of a person's life where they are more defined by the acts of sin. It is contrary and opposite to God's way of living. It's the act of not regarding God's guidelines for holy living.

Learner —learning a subject or skill and utilizing *God's word in their life.*

Led —*to be prompted, instructed, and directed by the Holy Spirit—He leads our way.*

Legalism is a set of laws above the Gospel, emphasizing a system of rules and regulations for achieving salvation and spiritual growth, opposite *God's grace.*

Lessons —period of teaching, tutoring of the *Holy Spirit by God's word.*

Life —Living Intentionally For Eternity, *the culmination of our real life in Christ.*

Lifestyle —the way one lives, an *influenced behavior by the flesh or Spirit.*

Light —*the natural agent that stimulates light, brightness, the ray of Christ's Light in us.*

Lineage —ancestry, family, heritage, roots, background, bloodline, *succession.*

Listener —*an attentive, intentional person who listens, hears, and applies God's word.*

Living Out —*the strength of Christ's Spirit at work within us, illuminating His Joy.*

Love —undeniable longing for affection and *all-consuming passion of commitment to Christ.*

Lustful —overwhelming sinful desire, pleasing oneself, *no regard for consequences.*

Lying —untruthful, false, dishonest, deceptive, underhand, hollow-hearted, *spiritually ill.*

M

Magnify —*make something appear more prominent, maximize, amplify,* and *enhance His glory in you.*

Malicious —someone intending to harm; this *is evil intent — and not Christlike.*

Manage —*in charge of, control, take forward, and handle God's word in your daily life.*

Manipulate —control or influence someone unfairly, without scruples or *malicious maneuvering.*

Materialism —is a kind of worldliness where God is gradually pushed off into a small corner, and the *physical substance is more important than the spiritual matter.*

Maturity —developed, effective, and fruitful, *changed from pleasing self to pleasing God.*

Mindset —an established set of fixed and growing attitudes *based on what is going into the mind — could be the spiritual game—changer in our daily life.*

Mortal —a human being subject to death, *but if in Christ as their Savior, they are immortal.*

Mercy —pity, compassion, kindness, forgiveness, *withholding punishment deserved.*

Mercy Seat —the lid on top of the Ark of Covenant where God was supposed to be seated, and from this place, He would dispense mercy to man when the blood of the atonement was sprinkled there. Christ, Himself is designated as our "propitiation." All our sins are covered by means of His death and our response to Christ through our faith in Him. This ties together the Old and New Testament concepts regarding the covering of sin as exemplified by the mercy seat of God.

Mirror—*Spiritual* —*the transformed image of our new life — and look like Christ.*

Misled —*deceived by someone, led in the wrong direction, lacks wisdom.*

Motives —reason for doing something, not hidden, intention, motivation, *Godly purpose.*

Mourning —expressing deep sorrow for someone's death, grieving for, wailing, *temporary.*

N

Need —require something of a necessity, essential, *significant in our life, like Christ.*

Negative —no optimism, not desirable, pessimistic, bleak, harmful, *a spiritual detriment.*

Neglect —fail to care of properly, untended, abandoned, *forsake His righteous ways.*

Nurture —*care for* — *encourage the growth and development of the feeding of His word.*

O

Obedience —comply with an order, respectful, a duty, disciplined, *conforming to all His ways.*

Obligation —legally bound to perform a duty or personal responsibility; it is the *requirement to serve Him.*

Offering —voluntarily putting forward graciously; it is joyously *submitting a gift to Christ. It is our advancement to Him for His glory.*

Omnipotent —*unlimited power, able to do anything, Supreme, Most-High, invincible.*

Omnipresent —*present everywhere, infinite, boundless, immeasurable.*

Omniscient —*all-knowing, all-wise, and all-seeing.*

Opinion —a viewpoint or judgment formed about something, most notably those that *align with God's word.*

Opportunity —*chance, good time, occasion, moment, opening, option, go and seize* — *now.*

Opposition —one that opposes, combats, fights against, and antagonizes another for their belief in a cause, *such as the enemy and unbelieving world against Christians.*

Oppression —heavily weighed down in spirit, mind, or body, *but Jesus can set us free.*

Overcome —prevail, get the better of, beat, tame, subdue, *get over, solve, triumph over.*

P

Passover —commemorates the Hebrews' liberation from slavery in Egypt and the "passing over" of the forces of destruction and sparing of lives when the lamb's blood was marked on their doorposts. Christ can save us when we accept Him as Savior.

Past —gone by in time and no longer existing — *such as your sins when you accept Christ.*

Patience —*restraint, calm, tolerance, even temperedness, composed, kindness, tranquil.*

Peace —restful, free from disturbance, stillness, solitude, *lack of interruptions—rest in Him.*

Perception —ability to hear, see or be aware of something, *a notion of God's word.*

Perish —suffer death, expire, fall, *go the way of all flesh, be lost, eternal death.*

Persecution —hostility, ill-treatment, *unfairness, and cruelty over a prolonged period.*

Perseverance —determination, diligence, patience, resolve, steadfastness, and *commitment to Him.*

Perspective —view, outlook, position, interpretation, frame of mind, approach—*God's lens.*

Perpetual —never-ending, long-lasting, without end, but as *believers — permanently in Christ.*

Perversion is the distortion or alteration of someone living from the original design of God's creation. They are misrepresenting God's natural plan and into an absolute state of falsehood. This is not acceptable in the eyes of God.

Planning —*decide, arrange, organize, work out, and expect God's word to develop you.*

Plagues Spiritually —a contagious disease that causes distress, torture, and torment but can be *delivered and freed when we give our lives to Christ.*

Pleasing —feel happy, satisfied, pleasant, acceptable, enjoyable, and *delightful in Him.*

Pleasures —happiness, satisfaction, delight, gladness, contentment, *enjoy His provisions.*

Potential —*showing the capacity to develop into something, life in the making for God.*

Position —a situation, orientation, posture, attitude, *your place grounded in Him.*

Positive —optimism, confidence, *helpful, beneficial, cheerful, Godly encourager.*

Possession —*the ownership and control of God in us, proclaiming His excellencies.*

Power —*is an inherent characteristic of God, the Christian life is an empowerment from God, the same power that raised Christ from the dead indwells in believers today.*

Praise —a *wholehearted expression of approval, admiration, and commendation to Christ.*

Prayer —a precious avenue that God has provided where we can raise our hearts by talking to Him, communicating *all our thoughts, needs, and desires — it is an intentional act.*

Precept —*a principle or doctrine intended to regulate our behavior, such as God's word.*

Predestined —*it is the biblical doctrine that God, in all His sovereignty, chooses specific individuals to be saved, but the choice to accept Him is "always available for anyone."*

Preparation —devise, put together, get ready, train, educate, discipline, *Godly grooming.*

Prepare —*get into spiritual shape, equip oneself with the Armor of God, and put in action.*

Pressures —an unavoidable part of life on earth, a squeezing and crushing— is the application of any power, but as believers in Jesus Christ, He relieves us from these forces.

Pride —a sinful, arrogant, haughty, self-reliant attitude or spirit that causes a person to have an inflated or puffed—up view of themselves, *Kingdom Killer.*

Priests —A chosen leader who can draw near to God and minister. He alone is responsible for offering divinely appointed sacrifices to God, executing the different procedures and ceremonies relating to God's worship, and representing God and man. Still, today *our Mediator is Jesus Christ.*

Priority —*something significant that we care about, like our time in His Word*— regarded or treated as more important, first concern, *greatest importance.*

Procrastinate —*put off, delay, undecided, take one's time, tactic, hesitate, spiritually lazy.*

Produce —make, build, put together, assemble, process, *mass—produce for His glory.*

Progress —*moving forward, advancing, and making headway in our daily Christian life.*

Promise —One declaring they will do exactly what they say, *such as God's plans for our salvation and blessings to His people.*

Propitiation —appeasing the wrath of sinners—*reconciled to God because of Christ's sacrifice.*

Protector —One Who defends or shields from injury, evil, and oppression.

Provide —make available for use, supply, assign, present; He *bestowed for our service.*

Provider —God supplies the needs of all creation but gives special care to his own people.

Pruning —*cut away things in our spiritual life that are unproductive and hinder growth.*

Purging —*to purify and separate us from dirty things in our lives.*

Purify —cleanse, refine, freshen, *strain contaminants, sift, and make pure by God.*

Purpose —the reason something is done, *a Christlike desire to achieve a good and righteous outcome.*

Pursue —follow someone, go after, run after, chase, *proceed along His path constantly.*

Q

Quality —the degree of excellence, standard, condition, character, worth, and *Godly values.*

R

React —behave in a particular way, retaliate, oppose, revolt against, *conduct oneself.*

Reality —*the real world, the Godly truth of His existence at work in our real life.*

Rebellion —*an act of violent resistance, civil disobedience, disorder, unrest, or anarchy.*

Receptive —willing to consider and accept *the quality of receiving the Truth of His word.*

Recognize —*identity, acknowledge an area of concern, and gain support from the Lord.*

Redemption —the *act of being saved from sin; God paid it all through His Son—Jesus Christ.*

Reformed —*changed from worse to better* — *when we allow His Spirit to work in us.*

Refuge —a condition of being safe or sheltered from pursuit, haven: *He is our everyday security.*

Refuse —one who is unwilling to do something, rejected as worthless, *spiritual defeat.*

Rejection —refuse something that could be of benefit, *a danger to deny the truth of God.*

Rejoice —*feeling of unbelievable joy, transporting that delight back to the ears of God.*

Relationship —*connection, bond, relevance, association, be a part of God's family.*

Religion —*belief and worship of the One True God, genuine godliness in practice, performing all duties to God and our fellow believers, in obedience to His divine command.*

Remembrance —reminding ourselves of all God has done for us in Christ.

Remove —cut off, detach, *and separate ourselves from anything, not Christlike.*

Renewed —*a new person, restored life, spiritually new, a new creation in Christ as Lord.*

Repent —*change one's mind and attitude, purpose from a course of alarming conduct to God.*

Repetition —*repeating something, copying, quoting God's word daily.*

Representative —*characteristic illustrative, an exemplary of Christlikeness in our life.*

Reproach —*find unacceptable, object to, dislike, or be against, such as false teachings.*

Reprobate —an evildoer, wretched person, worthless, *and unacceptable to God.*

Reputation —a belief held about someone, overall quality recognized by others, *is the opinion of others, Christ, in you?*

Resolve —settle, find a solution to a problem, *sort out, clarify, and set right in His sight.*

Response —something said or done to react to something – *a productive answer.*

Responsibility —*Godly duty to deal with something that needs to be made right—lovingly.*

Rest —*a refreshed and recharged spirit when grounded and dependent upon the Lord.*

Results —the outcome, findings, effects, *the by-products of His fruits at work in our life.*

Resurrection —*a rising again— a return from death to life— as the resurrection of Christ, it is strength for today — and bright hope for tomorrow.*

Reunion —*a reuniting after separation, our glorious reconnection with fellow believers.*

Reverence —*high esteem, deep respect, our favor, worship, honor, and praise to God.*

Rewards —*Our Lord recompenses us out of His kindness in return for well— done services.*

Righteousness —morally correct, the highest honor, justifiable, rightness, *acceptable — Christ.*

Role —*our part and character on this earth that should display Christlike qualities.*

S

Safeguard —a measure taken to protect someone, a provision; our *buffer is Jesus Christ.*

Salvation —*being delivered, by God's grace, from sin and its consequence of eternal punishment and being raised to newness of life in Christ Jesus.*

Saved —*rescued and delivered* from the hands of the enemy and eternal death.

Sanctified —*to be set apart from the world and used for God's holy work.*

Satan —accuser, destroyer, deceiver, manipulator, liar, enemy, prince of evil spirits, *the adversary of God and Christ.*

Satisfied —meet the expectations, needs, or desires of pleased, *content with all of God.*

Sealed —*to guarantee security and indicate our authentic ownership of God in us.*

Seek —an attempt to find something, pursue it—chase after it, *a relentless quest for God.*

Self-Control —the *ability to control self in emotions, desires, words, and deeds, a Godly fruit.*

Selflessness —*more concerned with the needs and well—being of others than themselves.*

Selfishness —the excessive concern for oneself, *their advantage, and pleasure.*

Sensitivity —*aware of the needs and emotions of others, responds with Christlikeness.*

Sensuality —*enjoyment or pursuit of physical pleasure, a carnal passion of ungodliness.*

Servant —one who performs duties for others, *a selfless helper in all facets.*

Service —helping someone, *genuine Christlike kindness — keeps one in good condition.*

Shameful —causing disgrace, embarrassing, dishonorable, *Christ can remove all shame.*

Sharing —have a portion with another, participate in *our Christlike fellowship with others.*

Shrewd —clever, *calculating,* sharp-witted, canny, wise, *it is another enemy's mask.*

Sight —the ability to see, visual perception, observe and *make out the truth.*

Significant —*sufficiently of foremost importance, worthy of,* notable —like Christ in us.

Sin —wicked, morally wrong, fallen, unholy, tainted, impure, *failure to do what is right.*

Slander —a false statement damaging to a person; it is malicious lying, and *God hates it.*

Slave *Spiritual* —the "possession" of his master, in obedience to his commands, *their actions signify ownership — the flesh or the Spirit.*

Slow —*designed to do so unhurriedly, deliberately, unrushed, relaxed, comfortably, steadily, and quickly, a gentle approach in many cases spiritually driven.*

Sly —conniving, scheming, deceitful, *manipulative, sneaky, an enemy masquerade.*

Solidity —the quality of being firm or strong in structure, *your steadfastness in Christ.*

Sovereignty —*Supreme Authority, Power, Dominion, and Control.*

Speech —the ability to express inner thoughts; it *is the utterance of good or bad things.*

Spiritual —*living out God's presence in our life — in a way that glorifies Him.*

Spiritual *Leader* —*a servant who influences people to think, say and behave in ways that enhance their spiritual life to discipleship and service for the Lord.*

Standards —quality level, excellence worth, guideline, benchmark, *God's requirement.*

Steadfastness —*is your firm and unwavering faith in the Lord so that nothing can deter you.*

Steps —the act of movement, in stride, course of action, strategy, *an initiative to follow God.*

Steward —*a man's relationship to God, identifies God as owner — and man as a manager.*

Storm —*a rushing, raging, or violent agitation used to mature and strengthen* Christlikeness.

Strategy —an approach designed to achieve an overall aim, *a grand design of Christlikeness.*

Strengthen —become more assertive, to add, *increase* an obligation or authority.

Stronghold —*see Foothold.*

Stubborn —unwilling to change attitude or position, *inflexible, bull-headed, pigheaded.*

Stumbling Block —a thing or someone *who keeps another from a relationship with God.*

Submission —*obedient to Authority and the very act of submitting to them for control.*

Success —the outcome of an aim or purpose, *a victory when we yield to God's guidance.*

Suffering —hardship, distress, tribulation, pain, agony, sadness, *not for long as believers.*

Surrender —*choose to give up the fight between self and God and surrender to His will.*

T

Tabernacle —was the center of worship of Yahweh by the people of Israel shortly after the Exodus. It housed the ark of the covenant, representing God's presence and serving as a place of sacrifice and worship.

Talents —*gifts from God in the form of a person's calling or natural ability — glorify Him.*

Task —work *to be done, duty, responsibility, and charge—such as the Great Commission.*

Teaching —*is one of the gifts of the Holy Spirit, the ability to explain God's Word clearly, and instruct and communicate knowledge as it relates to the faith and truths of the Bible.*

Temptation —the desire or urge to do something *wrong or unwise.*

Ten Commandments —the moral law given to Moses provided the foundation for a new Israelite society. Jesus called people to an even higher standard by obeying the commandments not only in their actions but also in their hearts.

Tension —stress, anxiety, nervousness, agitation, pressure, *restlessness, uncertainty.*

Test —a *challenging situation that prompts us to discern how God would have us respond.*

Thankfulness —*should be a way of life, naturally flowing from our hearts and mouths every day – because God is worthy.*

Thoughts —*an idea produced by thinking of an image can be good or bad, depending on what we are feeding into our minds that can make something pure or impure.*

Time —an allotted or used moment that *can yield a negative or positive experience.*

Tithing —*a joyful, voluntary giver who trusts God* as the source of all He's given them to supply their needs — *they are a cheerful giver, giving back portions of God's blessings.*

Together —in alliance, bonded as one, cooperate, partners, *in one accord with God.*

Tolerance —allow and accept an occurrence or practice, *ensuring it aligns with Scripture.*

Tongue—*Spiritual* —*it is either honoring the Lord or spewing venom that God forbids.*

Transformed —changed, altered, reshaped, renewed, remade, *and made to be used.*

Transparent —see-through, uncloudy, clearly exposed, *real Christlikeness seen in you.*

Trial —a cause of great suffering, *cross to bear, but God will give us strength.*

Trust —*a bold, confident, sure of security; it is what we do because of the faith we're given; it is Godly trust that will not waiver because it is based on faith in the promises of God.*

Truth —the quality of our *factual, genuine, authentic, and valid position in Christ.*

Turn Away —move or face a different location, and *your shift from ungodliness to godliness.*

U

Unbeliever —someone who has rejected Jesus Christ and wants nothing to do with Him, but Christ wants something to do with you because He cares. [insert smiley face]

Unchanging —*someone not changing, staying the same, caught in the enemy's trap.*

Understanding —*perceive God's word with intended and accurate meaning so you can live a true intentional life for God today.*

Unforgiveness —a *solid unwillingness* to restore what is broken, like taking poison and expecting someone else to die, *a spiritual killer, He forgave — so we can forgive.*

Unholy —ungodly, godless, depraved, sinful, wicked *with no room in God's Kingdom.*

United —joined together for *a common purpose or familiar feeling with the Lord daily.*

Unity —joined as a whole, unified, *a oneness with God, identity, selfsameness.*

Unrest —*dissatisfaction, disturbed, and agitation when the Lord's absent.*

Urgent —immediate action, desperate, *a severe cry for God's help in a dire situation.*

Usefulness —*superior quality of having utilities —gifts —that bring value to God.*

Utilize —*make practical and effective use of, deploy, and bring into action for God.*

V

Valid —well-founded, sound, defendable, robust, dependable, *convincingly Christlike.*

Value —*level of something deserved, important, worthy, like our daily steps with God.*

Verify —*make sure, demonstrate, justify, authenticate, confirm,* and *substantiate Him in us.*

Victory —is *that place in our relationship with God because He gives us the advantage or power over spiritual enemies, temptations, or any struggle in life. In Christ, we have the ultimate victory and the power of His indwelling Spirit alive and at work in us daily.*

Violence —force intended to hurt, damage, or kill, cruel, brutal, *no spiritual control.*

Vital —necessary, essential, fundamental, needed, *highest priority, such as His word alive in us.*

W

Wait —*to stay for— rest or remain still in expectation of— wait for orders; it is the power of undeniable willingness and patience "in His strength" to get you to the next phase.*

Walking —*move regularly, accompany, guide, and move in stride with Christ daily.*

Want —a desire to possess, care for, crave, thirst for, desperate, *a yearning for Christ.*

Warning —*Caution against danger, faults, or evil practices that can lead us astray.*

Weakness —*means we do not have what it takes, and we desperately need God daily.*

Weariness —*the weight of the world and exhaustion of everyday life leads us to this overly debilitating state, so we need God as our focal point to help balance this life.*

Wealth —*Spiritual —God's intelligence and wisdom in our life and His knowledge of truth and good, but true wealth is eternal life in Christ.*

Wholly —*entirely all in without any reservation, and to the maximum extent for the Lord.*

Wilderness Spiritually —an uninhabited area where we spend time alone and encounter God. It has a purpose and plans in our life with meaning and real-life application.

Willing —ready, eager, prepared, intend, desire, order, command, *a want of Him in you.*

Wisdom —having experience, wise, knowledgeable, discerning, *Godly judgment.*

Witness —*someone who boldly and confidently conveys to the world the evidence of what Jesus Christ did to transform their life into a faithful and serving Believer.*

Worship —*that feeling of complete reverence and adoration for our Lord and King.*

Worry —*spiritual defeater that accomplishes nothing. However, Christians do not worry, for they trust God wholly.*

Worthy —*deserving merits, excellence in qualities, an important person like Christ.*

Y

Yearning —an intense longing for something, craving, hunger, the *eagerness of Him—now.*

Yielding —submissive, inclined to give in, compliant, *a person who is bendable to God.*

Yoke —*the weight of a task or obligation— if joined with the right and most effective partner, it goes in a direction that will yield a very productive Christlike result.*

Z

Zeal —incredible energy, enthusiasm, love, devotedness, appetite, vigor, and *a solid and undeniable passion for Him in my life today.*